INFANTRY TACTICS

AND

MODERN WEAPONS.

1897

A TACTICAL AND PSYCHOLOGICAL STUDY
containing suggestions for the solution of the Attack.

TRANSLATED FROM THE GERMAN

with a proposed adaptation of the Author's Scheme to the British Infantry Attack

BY

P. H.

ALLAHABAD
PRINTED AT THE PIONEER PRESS

The Naval & Military Press Ltd

Published by the
The Naval & Military Press
in association with the Royal Armouries

Unit 10 Ridgewood Industrial Park,
Uckfield, East Sussex, TN22 5QE
Tel: +44 (0) 1825 749494
Fax: +44 (0) 1825 765701

In reprinting in facsimile from the original, any imperfections are inevitably reproduced and the quality may fall short of modern type and cartographic standards.

CONTENTS.

TRANSLATOR'S NOTE.

THIS essay, although undoubtedly very ably written, was in its original form unnecessarily complicated. Every effort has therefore been made to condense the translation, while at the same time taking every precaution against missing the author's leading points of argument.

In his anxiety to convict his readers, the author has "harped" too much upon certain fixed ideas.

It should be further observed that, from the title of the paper, no idea is given that a definite "scheme of attack" has been formulated.

In his crusade against the theory of the "attack" as at present generally accepted throughout the Armies of Europe, he does not include the English system. It strikes one, however, as quite possible that many of his valuable hints might profitably be included in the present English Drill Book.

The great simplicity of his system is at once apparent. It is based on the principle of "extended order," a principle which permeates the English "attack" formation more than that adopted by any other army.

The hints as regards *practical* company training, the importance of "cover" being subordinated to tactical consideration, and of combining "fire" and "movement" during the attack, are especially worthy of notice.

His remarks regarding the study of Military history, and "applied" tactics are also very much to the point, for, although he claims that modern weapons have put recent campaigns, as *Tactical models*, out of date, he points out the usefulness of their study, with a view to finding out why and where errors were committed, and so guarding against their recurrence.

Infantry must be independent and capable of self-defence to the uttermost and, until we recognize that, the author considers, our "Tactical methods" can never be healthily developed.

He shews most clearly the symptoms of weakness, in the present "attack," and claims the removal of these symptoms by the adoption of a formation such as he proposes. This formation, though containing the elements of "normal" organization, is by no means of the nature of a sealed pattern, and enables the "attack" to develop great frontal strength with great depth, whilst obtaining the utmost possible fire effect, and at the same time minimizing that of the enemy. The system is *most* elastic and can be adapted to any kind of ground or circumstances.

Frontal strength, he maintains, will be of primary importance in a future campaign, and to this we must subordinate every other artifice designed with intent to shatter the "defence."

In connection with the author's remarks bearing on the "systems" of attack as adopted by the various European Armies in the present day, it is interesting to read General Bengough's valuable little work on Tactics,* in which he describes the French attack formation which is to a certain extent analogous with that proposed by

* "Thoughts on Tactics" by Major-General Bengough, C.B., Chapter V. Infantry, p. 28.

the author. In the same work will be found an interesting account of some experiments carried out at Okehampton in 1895. These go far to support the author's statements regarding the value of his formation when Infantry are exposed to modern Artillery fire. Unfortunately, however, in the account of these experiments, no range is given.

It will be seen from a perusal of Chapter III., of General Bengough's work, that he holds somewhat widely different opinions to the author as to the scope and possibilities of Cavalry reconnaissance.

It is, however, worthy of note that General Bengough calls attention, in his chapter upon Infantry,* to the necessity of having, if not some "rigid normal formation," at least some tactical organization that can be adapted to the "*ever-varying conditions of a tactical situation.*" One is forcibly struck with the truth of these remarks, when one considers that in our own army, the systems adopted by even different units are so widely different in detail, that if called upon to act in concert, the relation of strength to frontage and a host of other considerations of vital importance in delivering an attack on a large scale would fail to exist.

At the very commencement of this little book, General Bengough further observes that the present time is undoubtedly opportune for a careful revision of our state of preparedness for war.

Whilst working out various problems based on the system proposed by the author, it has struck me that it would adapt itself in every possible way to what General

---

* See pp. 29, &c.

Bengough terms the "keystone of tactics," *i.e.*, "section command," since the British company of hundred rifles would form the four "ranks" or "lines" advocated, and, as I have endeavoured to shew, each section would remain intact from start to finish of the attack.

Indeed, as regards details of drill and manœuvre from one to another of the proposed formation, the system would appear to adapt itself even better to ours, than to the German drill.

In an appendix, therefore, I have attempted to shew, by the aid of rough diagrams, how these formations would be adopted both by a company and a battalion.

I have further shewn a German battalion attacking on the proposed system, as also the frontage and depth occupied by German and British battalions and brigades respectively.

As an aid in studying this translation it is of interest to read an article, which appeared in the *Journal of the United Service Institution of India*, April 1896, entitled "The German, French, and Russian systems of Infantry attack and defence." It is a comparison of the existing regulations in the three armies. For easy reference, I append the following extract :—

"The main ideas are practically analogous in the three armies, the principles being roughly as follows :—

(*a*) Whenever possible a flank as well as a frontal attack should be carried out.

(*b*) Development of a sufficiently strong firing line at the right moment.

(*c*) All available fire to be concentrated on the defenders at effective distances, every advantage being taken of the ground over which the advance is made.

(*d*) As soon as firing has commenced, the line to be re-inforced as required, the advance being carried out gradually, and every effort made to gain preponderance of fire.

(*e*) Reserve to be kept as far as possible out of range of the enemy's fire from the commencement, but to be gradually and steadily advanced, until they are eventually brought up rapidly into the firing line, when the whole will advance to the assault.

(*f*) This must be followed up by fire brought to bear upon the retreating enemy, the reconcentration of troops, the pursuit being then carried out either by patrols or whole corps as may be directed.

"The actual system of attack differs in some details in the various armies.

"No 'normal attack' is recognized by the Germans, the outline merely being given, and the rest being left to the discretion of commanders, the guiding principle being that a well delivered and determined attack ensures success.

"The following are the most characteristic points in the German system:—

i. Unless ordered to the contrary, skirmishers extend at an interval of 1-2 paces between files. The frontage occupied by a company in the fighting line will, however, not exceed 100 mètres (108 yards), as the extension of entire companies is generally delayed until the last stages of the attack.

ii. At the commencement of the attack not more than ¼ of the whole will, as a rule, be extended, and not less than ¼ kept in reserve. This is, however, not a hard and fast rule.

iii. The distance of units in rear of the fighting line varies according to requirements from 200 mètres (219 yards) upwards.

iv. Skirmishers are only to double over open ground, and when the enemy's fire renders it necessary.

v. On reaching the zone of effective fire, troops in close formation form single rank, but there is no hard and fast rule as regards intervals.

vi. On the signal "alert" denoting the approach of Cavalry, the square formation is only adopted when the Infantry have been demoralized, and ammunition is running out, or when retiring over open country, and continually being harassed by large bodies of Cavalry.

vii. There are two kinds of fire employed according to the regulations, *viz.*, "volleys" and "independent."* Volleys are usually employed at the commencement of the attack when the firing line is not within effective range of the enemy's fire, and are therefore the exception, and not the rule.

* German, "Schützenfeuer" *lit.* "skirmishers or marksmen's fire."

viii. At the closer ranges, and up to 600 mètres (650 yards), everything is aimed at, at the medium ranges, and up to 1,000 mètres (1,080 yards) at high and wide objects, and only exceptionally at the long ranges over 1,000 mètres (1,080 yards) at large and deep formations. From 800 mètres (866 yards) upwards, when the range cannot be approximately fixed, two sight vanes 100 mètres apart are used.

ix. Rapid firing is as a rule only employed when within 350 mètres (380 yards) of the position, but in exceptional cases it may be used effectively up to 1,000 mètres (1,080 yards).

x. Firing "on the move" seldom has any effect, and is therefore scarcely ever employed, except when perhaps a skirmishing line is retiring and is hard pressed by the enemy. Similarly long range indirect fire is seldom employed. Such are the complete details of the attack as laid down, innovations being strictly prohibited by the regulations."

The appendix will also shew some of the main general points to be considered with regard to the adoption of the proposed system.

I should like to take this opportunity of expressing my gratitude to those who have so kindly perused and criticised this compilation in the rough, and who have favoured me with their valuable opinions and criticisms.

The main object in submitting this work to the public, has been to invite discussion on a matter so vitally important to the interests of every modern army.

P. H.

31*st March* 1897.

THE MORAL AND MATERIAL EFFECT OF MODERN ARMS OF PRECISION UPON INFANTRY TACTICS.

AUTHOR'S INTRODUCTORY NOTE.

The meaning of the term "Tactics."

THE title which I have chosen for this paper embraces so wide and intricate a field of military science, that it will be perhaps as well if I offer a few explanatory observations. *

By "Tactics" I mean the various methods or systems adopted by Infantry during an engagement, and these methods are naturally of two distinct classes, *viz.*, those of a positive and those of a negative nature.

By the former are meant those tactical methods by which fire-arms are most effectively and successfully employed, and inflict the severest possible damage on an enemy, while by the latter are meant those tactical methods best adapted to secure immunity to one's own force from the effect of an enemy's weapons.

Now it is obvious that since both methods are diametrically opposed to one another, the great art lies in a skilful and successful combination of both.

With modern arms of precision a force which seeks only to attain positive results may itself be

---

* The literal title of the paper is—"The system of Infantry fighting before the judgment seat of modern weapons."—*(Translator.)*

decimated within a very short period, more especially if advancing to attack over open ground. Should only negative results be aimed at, then indeed all possible chances of success are gone.

The present difficulties in "Tactics."

Thus we find ourselves in a tactical dilemma, the mastery of which may rank as the most difficult task we have ever been asked to accomplish.

Turning to ancient history, we find that each fighting formation had its own peculiar national characteristics, witness the old Greek Phalanx, the Roman Legion, the Germanic "Wedge" formation, &c., &c.

Development of "Tactics" from the earliest times.

As fire-arms were invented and improved, and as, with the advance of civilization, nations were brought into closer contact, these national characteristics gradually disappeared, until at the present time we find that the systems of "attack" and "defence" employed by all nations are almost identical. In practically every system of "attack," the formation adopted is that of so-called "loose" or "open order" (*l'ordre dissolu*). The principle is one of thin "double-rank columns" with "skirmisher swarms."

Roughly speaking, then, these are the formations in which Infantry now trust to use their own weapons, with the utmost effect, and at the same time suffer the minimum loss from the fire of the enemy, and the direct responsibility for their adoption lies with the breech-loader and its destructive power. It was first employed in 1866, but by the Prussians only, and with what results is well known. In 1870, breech-loader met breech-loader, but in spite of the great superiority of the French weapon, the Germans more than compensated for it by their Artillery.

All armies are now, practically speaking, equally well armed, but so enormously have fire-arms been improved, that there is no comparison between those of the present day and those used in 1870. Yet, in spite of this important fact, our system is the same as it was in those days.

Although it is my intention to point out the defects of this system, I would like it to be clearly understood that I am not stigmatizing any special system, and that in my humble estimation, considering the conditions obtaining at the time of their issue, the German Drill Regulations are as nearly perfect as possible.

Yet as time goes on, improvements are made almost from day to day, and inaction means retrogression in everything pertaining to human science and knowledge.

When the problems raised by the improvements in fire-arms are satisfactorily solved, we shall be the first to reap the benefit, and my sole object in writing this essay has been to suggest some possible solution of so difficult a question.

Effect of fire-arms upon "Tactics."

When fire-arms were first introduced, the idea gradually gained ground that the "defence" was the easier and the "attack" the more "difficult" of accomplishment, and as time went on, and fire-arms were improved, this idea was still further strengthened. Coming down to the present day, we find that the Infantry "attack" is the most difficult operation within the region of Tactics. More than this, it is accepted as a sort of "Article of faith" that under fire of the "defence" the assailant is absolutely debarred from advancing; in short, that the "defence" is unassailable. And yet why? The strength of the defence is purely material, its weakness traceable directly to moral influences, whereas for the assailants matters are exactly reversed. Which then has the power of improving the position ? Surely the assailant only, the " defence " *never*.

It is an accepted axiom all the world over, that the attack has been enormously weakened by the introduction of modern fire-arms whilst the defence has thereby been strengthened to an unlimited extent. I must protest that this is merely a traditional error, and shall give my reasons for this later. I shall for the present confine myself to observing that it is not that the attack, *as such*, has lost strength, but only in proportion to the effect of the modern rifle, simply because our present tactical methods are exactly the same as they were when the first breech-loader was introduced, a circumstance which, moreover, does not affect the defence to the same extent.

Since the war of 1870-71 and 1877-78, all armies have been busily engaged in studying the art of Tactics, and in revising and altering their respective regulations, shewing what a prevailing spirit of rivalry and competition exists in preparing for the next great war.

It will be my greatest reward, if I have in any measure stimulated this spirit of rivalry in the interests of our own splendid army, for which I maintain only the " best " can be good enough. I must leave it to others to decide as to the truth of my conviction.

I have avoided any attempt to convince my readers by mere rhetorical effect, preferring to stick to plain unvarnished expression of my ideas just as they have occurred to me.

CHAPTER I.

In the second part of the German Drill Book of 1888, which deals with the "battle," everything in the nature of a "normal system" or "scheme" has been entirely omitted.

The volume is particularly distinguished by its inauguration of "adapted" * or "applied" tactics, in the place of "normal" tactics; in other words, a system of "confidence" † or "trust" instead of one of "mistrust." ‡ Indeed, this idea of "confidence in leadership" is noticeable throughout the regulations.

"Normal" and "adapted" Tactics.

Among those, however, who are searching after truth within the sphere of tactical knowledge, there are two leading parties whose principles are diametrically opposed to one another, and between which, it will be exceedingly difficult to effect a reconciliation. The one is striving to attain a tactical prototype, that is to say, a stable *tactical frame-work,* whilst the other maintains that the only practical solution of the question is to be found in the evolution of tactics in each individual case; in fact, what I have referred to above as "adapted" tactics. § Now it seems to me that this is altogether the wrong way to attempt a solution of so difficult a problem, as the new rifle (Model '88) has set us. This weapon was not introduced until after the issue of the drill book, and could not therefore have been

* German, "Taktik nach Umständen."

† "Taktik des Vertrauens."

‡ "Taktik des Misstrauens."

§ It is difficult to express these terms satisfactorily in English.—(*Translator.*)

considered when framing the regulations, which were based mostly on the experiences of the 1870-71 war, and the performances of the 1871—84 rifle.

The following brief summary may serve to shew how vastly superior the new rifle is to the old one:—

Description of the modern rifle.

The most essential point of difference lies in the employment of smokeless powder, thus rendering the "defence" far easier, and giving the attack every disadvantage. These advantages and disadvantages are so universally known, that it will suffice for me to observe, that whereas formerly it was impossible for the defenders, however well posted, not to betray their position, it is now quite possible for the assailant to be under effective fire, without knowing whence such fire is coming, and thus rendering the discovery of the defenders' position a matter of extreme difficulty.

With the old rifle it was frequently necessary for the defenders to cease fire with a view to taking fresh aim and clearly observing the movements and dispositions of the assailants. Now all movements of the assailants must be made under fire, and in clear view, of the defenders, rendering the advance likewise a matter of great difficulty.

The '88 rifle has an extremely flat trajectory and consequently is effective over a larger area out of all proportion to the old rifles. The elevation, for instance, at 500 mètres (about 550 yards) is only 1·50 mètre (about 5 feet) or less than a man's height, whereas with the old rifle it was almost 10 feet. Another advantage is it's marvellous precision. The deviation, for example, at 600 mètres (660 yards), is only 64 centimètres (about 25 inches) while with the old rifle it was almost double that.

Its penetration is so great that several men can be hit standing one behind the other, while the thicknesses of earth, wood, stone, etc., hitherto considered protective, are now quite inadequate.

Its effective range is about 800 mètres, (about 870 yards), whilst rapidity of fire has been also greatly increased.

Now although the assailants will undoubtedly to a certain extent reap the benefit of these improvements, we cannot deny the immense advantages given to the defence, and must confess that an Infantry attack is one of the most difficult problems of the future.

The relation of modern fire-arms to "normal" and "adapted" systems.

It is quite obvious, moreover, that this immense improvement in fire-arms, combined with the fact that strategy must pay forfeit to superior armament, puts all the strategical and tactical experience of 1870-71 entirely in the shade.

Until, therefore, the vastly important question of satisfactorily combining "positive" and "negative" results is settled, neither the advocates of "normal" nor "adapted" tactics can claim even existence for their methods.

In many instances it might be easier to attain the desired object by the adoption of a sound "normal" scheme, whilst, on the other hand, often the very best "normal" tactics might often lead to most inglorious results. There is a good example of this in the attack made by the Prussian Guards at St. Privat and the fighting at the "Mance" ravine. One individual case cannot justify the acceptance of a rule, and it is impossible to limit the art of war, with all its innumerable elments of chance, to hard-and-fast rules.

The supporters of the "normal" attack advocate the extension of *small* bodies of skirmishers during the first stage, with a *gradual* development, while those in favour of "adapted" tactics maintain that the only chance of success lies in the extension of large numbers of skirmishers from the very commencement, to the extent of whole regiments or even brigades. Recognizing the great difficulties of obtaining depth, they assert that the only possible alternative is to employ "masses" of skirmishers.

Let us call this then the "massed skirmisher system" * in contradistinction to that of the Drill Regulations which insist on economy of force, and reinforcement of the firing line from the rear, in other words a system of "fighting in depth."† Which, therefore, of the two systems is correct? We are reminded of the ever victorious "linear" tactics of the Great Frederick, and yet, on the other hand, we have Napoleon's system of "masses of skirmishers," and heavy massed columns, while as the greatest authority on modern warfare and the greatest hero of modern military history, we have von Moltké; who therefore shall decide? I think it must be confessed that our only and wisest councillor to start with, is the "bullet of the future."

The subject has been most diligently and carefully studied from its very foundation. No stone has been left unturned in gleaning the true from the false. In writing this essay, I have taken our modern weapons as the main factors affecting the question of Tactics generally. I have further given the fullest consideration to history and

---

* German, "Schützenmassentaktik."

† German, "Kampf aus der tiefe"=lit. fighting from depth.

science, and yet I would wish it understood from the very commencement how thoroughly I realise the immense difficulties attending my self-set task. The general question of the tactics of the future being as yet entirely unsolved, the subject must be naturally one of general or international interest, and I shall therefore endeavour to discuss the matter from as impartial a view as possible.

I have already mentioned that, with the exception of a few minor details, the system adopted by all armies is practically the same.

Description of the systems practised at present by European Armies.

The main fighting formation consists of a skirmishing "swarm" which is deployed from the double-rank company column. The sub-division of the company into three or four sections is immaterial.

This therefore is our present tactical unit with which we have to work, and on which all fighting formations must be based, it being impossible to improvise one on the spot. If, however, we were to attempt to adapt this system to larger bodies, or, in other words, to lay down a "sealed pattern" applicable to units of any size, we should indeed paralyse our commanders to such an extent, that they would become mere figure-heads, who must fail at the first real test.

It is of course absolutely essential that every unit, up to at least a brigade, should have some "method" which ensures simultaneous dispositions for the attack, and hence the present feverish desire to adopt some "normal" system. It has been recognized that "adapted" tactics cannot always achieve the desired object, indeed in an attack on a large scale, success might be seriously jeopardized, the weakest point in these "adapted" tactics being the system of bringing up supports which, though indispensible, disintegrates units to an alarming extent.

To attain this most desirable end, the first thing to be done is to evolve some kind of fundamental principle, applicable, in the first instance, to the *company*. It must be one that is fully adapted in every conceivable way, both actively and passively, to the requirements of modern fire-arms. And I feel sure it can be found if we only bear in mind the actual conditions of the battle-field, and examine the conditions of warfare from a scientific point of view. What do we mean by a "system?" Surely it is but a concrete development of intellectual and scientific reasoning. But it must justify its existence by its perfection, and by bearing the distinctive birth-marks of scientific research and experience. As, however, science has to base its researches on the effect of the weapons employed, these researches are of course just as liable to alteration as the weapons themselves, and this again entails a change in the system.

How to evolve a system.

However great the moral value of traditions may be in an army, they must give way before the march of science. Tradition and science are such discordant elements in "normal" tactics, that both can never be equally potent factors. The truth of this has been proved in military history a thousand times over.

Generally speaking these elements of tradition, warlike instinct, courage and discipline, to preserve which it is our most sacred duty, are not dependent on the tactical system adopted, that is; the system is not necessary to their existence. It is indeed possible that, with a system based on scientific principles, they may be developed to the utmost advantage.

If therefore our "system" is the concrete result of intellectual and scientific reasoning, and since every individual case deserves special treatment, surely each individual case deserves special study, and the results of these studies should give us some basis to work upon. I will now ask my readers to follow me in a brief historical retrospect.

Tactical Retrospect.

The "line," or "linear" tactics of Frederick the Great were based on a "normal" system. This consisted in a tactically sound process of deployment, and in those days was accepted as "fire tactics" *par excellence.*

The whole of the Infantry were drawn up in two lines of equal strength, at about 300 paces distance. This formation was adopted when about 1,500 paces from the enemy, and the whole then advanced at a steady slow pace shoulder-to-shoulder.

At about 300 paces fire was opened, and it was invariably found that, provided the troops continued the advance after coming under fire—always a matter of extreme difficulty, the enemy retreated before it came to hand-to-hand fighting.

The great difficulty lay in the officers being able to control their men and induce them to advance—a fact in ancient history that is most instructive for us, since it is now more imperative than ever to combine "fire" with "movement." Applying therefore the above historical facts to modern warfare, we should find something of the following nature :—

Massed formations unsuitable under the fire of modern rifles.

'"Skirmisher Masses" cannot advance without having previously silenced the fire of the defenders. Should they come under the fire of the latter advance is impossible."'

If therefore we imagine that the system of "masses of skirmishers" will enable us to carry out an attack under the fire of modern rifles, surely we are "*following a phantom.*" Even had we ten times as many troops as the enemy, we should fail. It matters little whether we employ "massed" skirmishers or "massed" columns, we are merely offering a greater sacrifice to the modern breech-loading "Moloch." Massed fire from a defensive position has now been rendered almost annihilating in its effect, and beyond the final zone (350 mètres), it will be impossible for the assailants to silence it by the employment of "masses." It is merely adding fresh fuel to the fire. The only practicable system is one by which picked men can advance in such a formation as will render the enemy's fire ineffectual.

To prove this we have only to go to the range. Let the targets represent the assailants, and be made in the shape of men standing. Open fire at 600 yards and upwards, with a line of skirmishers extended at 2—3 paces. Then carry out the same experiment on a compact swarm covering the same frontage, shoulder-to-shoulder, or "skirmisher masses," and then count the hits. Then reverse the case.

Recognizing only too well the difficulties attending offensive action by Infantry, with its conflicting elements of fire and movement, and failing, moreover, in a successful combination of them to the same extent as we have in the present day, the Great Frederick adopted the only alternative, he fixed bayonets, and the Gordian Knot was cut. Even then, however, he often failed, whilst with modern fire-arms we should be simply mad to attempt it. Indeed, the situation is now reversed, for we have to concentrate our heaviest fire and prevent the use of the bayonet.

This, however, brings us no nearer to the solution of the main question.

With the French revolution we enter upon yet another phase. Napoleon trusted to his Artillery for "fire," and to his Infantry for "movement." At "Aspern" he suffered his first decisive defeat, while at Waterloo his massed attack on the English lines was equally disastrous, resulting in the utter route of his whole army. And yet at that time fire effect was a mere bagatelle to what it is now. It was but the natural retribution following a direct transgression of all the rules and principles of Infantry tactics. These may be summed up in the two words "extended order"; "*masses*," as such, are rather of political and strategical importance.

CHAPTER II.

THE international politics of the present day render it imperative to employ enormous bodies of men, and this quantity must be an increasing one. Every true politician and soldier must recognize the fact that without them it would be impossible to carry any vast strategical schemes into execution. Hence the present military system obtaining in Germany.

The evolution of tactics since the introduction of breech-loaders.

If we follow up the evolution of tactics since the introduction of the breech-loader, we shall scarcely be surprised to find that there has been a steadily increasing tendency to substitute "skirmishing lines" for "columns." This tendency was due to national causes. When armed with the breech-loader, the Prussian troops considered their lines invincible, and the absolute confidence they had in their weapon enabled them to assume the offensive on every possible occasion. This feeling of invincibility continued to increase, and indeed formed the basis of all tactical considerations.

Just before 1866, von Moltké said: "To increase the effect of rifle fire you must have clear view, knowledge of the distance, and steady firing."

We have not as many riflemen,* as rifles. Twenty or 30 good shots suffice to inflict very considerable loss upon an enemy under good cover. Supposing now that these are joined by 100 "tirailleurs" firing hurriedly and carelessly, and the

* German, "Schützen" = lit. skirmishers or marksmen.—*(Translator.)*

difference will be scarcely appreciable. Under normal conditions however, and in a *bataille rangée*, what will decide the issue is not so much marksmanship, as massed fire at distances where knowledge of the range is of less importance. To advance under such a fire, will certainly be exceedingly difficult, and a commander who succeeds in bringing his men up to within 300* paces of the enemy, may safely reckon on victory.

When advancing to attack over open ground and against a determined enemy, Infantry must of course waver. Some thirty years ago von Moltké said: "Commanders should remember that even the bravest troops in the world must waver before an insurmountable obstacle." Even then the Great General thoroughly disbelieved in the system of "massed skirmishers." Under modern rifle fire from 1,000 mètres onward the percentage of losses would be enormous, besides which we have to consider how immensely modern field works have been improved by obstacles.

Moral effect of improved weapons.

It has been lately asserted that Infantry engagements will be decided at between 700 and 500 mètres. If true, then the fate of the assailants is indeed sealed, for they cannot possibly gain preponderance of fire until they have advanced beyond that distance, and until then the defenders are masters of the situation. I must therefore denounce this assertion as most misleading, dangerous, and contrary to all logical reasoning.

Paradoxical though it may sound, it is a matter for congratulation that our soldiers' eyes have

* This distance has perhaps been increased owing to flat trajectory and great precision of the modern rifle. Even so, it may be taken at not more than 530 mètres (400 yards)—*Author.*

not improved in proportion to their rifles, a last remaining fact, one of which the assailant must and can make capital. But of this more anon. Now that armies are on fairly equal terms as regards both armament and numbers, the strategical and tactical lessons of 1870-71 are altogether out of date, though in future campaigns tactical knowledge will undoubtedly play an exceedingly important if not decisive part.

The basis of that strategy which sought to crush the foe by mere force of numbers, has however ceased to exist, while the "Infantry attack" will be the "tactical" *chef d'œuvre* of the future. Even as early as 1866, Prince Frederick Charles foretold the influence of improved weapons upon tactics, that is as regards "extension" and the disintegration of tactical units.

He most strongly impressed on all company commanders, and even more to battalion commanders, the urgent necessity of keeping their units in hand. Failing this, he added, combined action under their generals, one of the most essential factors in victory, would be rendered impossible. The events of 1866 proved the indisputable truth of his words, while in 1870, all our weak points were attributable to this same cause, and it is highly probable that history will repeat itself in an even more pronounced manner.

"Extended order" the result of the introduction of breech-loaders.

The introduction of the breech-loader was followed by the complete extension of all formations, which practically changed the whole aspect of the fight.

Captain May regarded this innovation as a basis for the foundation of a system adaptable to intelligent leadership.

His scheme of sending out whole companies in "swarms" supported by whole companies in the 2nd line was at that time regarded as phenomenal. Now it has been rendered absolutely necessary, we cannot pretend to claim that our present system has been made adaptable to it.

In May's opinion the strength of the Prussian Army lay in its supreme and subordinate commanders, its weakness in the generals and intermediate commanders. Now, although he was undoubtedly right in his estimate of the effect of breech-loaders upon tactics, in this particular point he unquestionably mistook cause for effect, *i.e.*, he attributed the defects of the system to individual incapacity.

The difficulties of control by subordinate commanders.

The present system of "skirmisher swarms" absolutely precludes general and intermediate commanders, and often even company commanders, from exercising any control at all, the only thing left to compensate for it being independent action on the part of subordinate officers. Now there is no doubt that independent action of this nature cannot attain its object unless it permeates the whole army, and is thoroughly *en rapport* with the intentions of those directing operations, a degree of perfection it is scarcely possible to attain, as I shall endeavour to shew later on.

Von Moltke's recognition of the danger attending "mass tactics."

Indeed von Moltké was well aware how dangerous the system of skirmisher swarms would prove if employed against a skilful and determined enemy such as we may reasonably expect to meet in the next war, for in a memorial addressed to His Majesty, he wrote as follows :—

"We must recognize the fact that our greatest fault in 1866 lay in the absence of perfect control by general officers over subordinate commanders.

"No sooner are the brigades and divisions launched in the attack, than all such control ceases. As a rule, we find that it is individual battalions and companies that distinguish themselves in action.

"With a skilful and determined enemy, however, we run most serious risks."

Reading between the lines it is easy to see that these defects were not attributable primarily at least to individual commanders, for in that case they would have been discovered and removed, and moreover the same defects were noticed throughout the whole army.

In 1870 the same mistakes occurred, with the exception that, as a rule, it was not the battalion but the company or even the section, that acted on its own initiative.

Applying, then, these lessons of the past to the great war of the future, what do we learn? Let us bear in mind the vast difference between our camps-of-exercise and the battle-field of the future.

The necessity of Infantry being independent.

It is an indisputable fact that the only possible way of delivering the actual assault is by effective fire at very close ranges. Long range fire is ineffective with the very best rifle, and there is and can be no alternative but to get as close as possible to the position. The only question is, how to reach this close range? To the obvious reply that "the Artillery must prepare the way," I would merely point out that the defenders' Artillery will have a very great deal to say on the subject before such a desirable object is attained. No one arm should be unconditionally dependent on the other, and Infantry least of all.

Battles in future must be decided at close ranges.

No greater error can be committed than that of opening fire too soon at long ranges; indeed, it has been said that a good general will never reply to heavy long range firing unless with a few picked shots who will, moreover, find the masses of the enemy a most excellent target to aim at. This is an important point which seems to have been entirely ignored at the present time.

What we have to discover then is a system which most effectually combined logical, tactical, and psychological principles.

Relationship of "flank" to "frontal" attacks.

It has been for a long time evident that the Infantry being of great frontal strength, demonstrates the possibility of flank attacks. The defenders, however, presumably know where their weak points lie just as much as the assailants, and unless the latter are numerically stronger (which is doubtful in a future campaign), they could still offer a stubborn resistance on any threatened flank. No turning movement will therefore affect the result of the action unless combined with an equally determined frontal attack. A flank attack should never be undertaken purely with a view of avoiding the difficulties of a frontal attack. Although I am fully aware of the value of flank attacks, and the great advantage of strategically out-manœuvring and demoralizing the defence, it is questionable whether the attacking force will in future have sufficient numbers available.

Disintegration of units under the present system.

I have already mentioned that in the war of 1870, the fire of breech-loaders was such as to cause considerable confusion, though of course there were individual exceptions. In order then to compensate for this disorganization, the present system provides for fresh units being improvised on the spot. Now,

Methods adopted to prevent it.

although fully recognizing the value of this method, I am of opinion that is nothing more nor less than giving medicine to a dying man, and Infantry tactics being therefore in the last stage of disease, the question is whether the "massed skirmisher" system is the only possible remedy.

The defects I have referred to would be scarcely of so much importance if they affected both "attack" and "defence" to an equal extent. Unfortunately, however, it is the "attack," whose weak points are material ones, that must suffer most.

Examples.

There is no better instance of the difficulties attending an Infantry attack than the action of St. Privat, where the regiments engaged in the frontal attack lost one-half of their officers, and one-third of their men, although we must of course be prepared for just as heavy losses in the present day.

An Army Order issued on 21st August, concluded as follows:—

"I expect officers so to bring their intelligence to bear that by thoroughly preparing for the attack and the adoption of suitable formations, success will in future be achieved with less loss."

The formation adopted was one of dense "swarms of skirmishers" supported by columns in rear, in other words, "massed formation," and although, as a rule, it was the columns that lost most heavily, the fact remains that the "swarms" did not reach the point they intended to. Even in those days any idea of massed formations was officially repudiated, and it was recognized, although perhaps only indirectly, that such formations were no longer practicable. Fighting in close formation is now altogether out of date, and the greater the numbers available the more carefully they should be employed. Every man and every rifle must be carefully husbanded, for unless the tactical situation imperatively demands it, any waste of men or ammunition will assuredly lead to serious consequences.

Let us take, for example, a brigade attacking in massed formation.

Frontage required by a brigade under the present system.

The six battalions are formed in one large mass of skirmishers. Anything closer than shoulder-to-shoulder is of course out of the question, for unless each man has free use of his rifle, both front and rear rank are merely sacrificed to no purpose.

A brigade would thus require a frontage of 6 kilomètres (about 3¾ miles), whereas we may be pretty sure that all the brigade could really occupy on a future battle-field would be about 1 kilomètre (1,093 yards). The skirmisher "mass" would in this case be six-deep, but assuming that at least four battalions are employed in the fighting line, and two battalions as Reserve, we may take it at four-deep. I will now ask my readers to just imagine what the advance of this brigade will be like, say at about 2,000 mètres (2,200 yards) from the enemy, over rough ground, or take the case of a brigade attacking with a front of 1,093 yards and imagine what it would be like, unless deep formation was adopted. Whatever the weapons, deep formation is the only natural and therefore the only practical fighting formation. All that is required is to adapt it to the rifle in use. In "linear" tactics (*i.e.*, fighting in single rank) there is neither tactical impetus nor moral force.

Manœuvres apt to be deceptive.

I am inclined to think that "mass Tactics" must have originated at manœuvres where regiments or brigades at peace strength, actuated by a desire to out-flank the position attacked, occupy a frontage out of all proportion to that which even brigades or divisions would actually occupy in the field. This is a point to which I shall return later on.

"Fire and Movement."

Turning to the attack of a brigade let us now consider the question of "fire and movement." As long as the fire of the defenders permits, the advance will continue. being extended, the assailants can open fire at any moment, and it is this fire which must decide the battle. Now it need scarcely be observed that it is extremely probable that fire will be opened too soon, and nothing paralyses or delays the action so much as long range fire. How then, when once firing has commenced, are we to give these "masses" the required impetus to resume the advance? Being, as it were, held-fast by the fire of the defenders, they cannot advance without some fresh moral stimulus.

Long range firing disastrous.

The more we extend the system of general conscription, and shorten the period of service, the more must we consider the moral qualities of the average soldier.

Why did the Prussian Guard, second to none as regards courage and discipline, pay such a heavy penalty to the 70-71 breech-loader? Why did they halt? And why could they not resume the advance? Did the French "skirmisher masses" ever succeed against our inferior rifles with their vastly superior ones? Take only one of many instances.

The failure of French swarms in 1870-71.

The 20th (French) Corps had advanced against Beaune la Rolande, and pushed the German outposts back into the town, where, except for two companies of the 57th, the only troops available were the three battalions of the 16th Regiment distributed equally along the three exposed sides. Dense masses of skirmishers surrounded the place, the buildings had been set on fire in several places, by the enemy's shells, and the churchyard wall had been breached. Yet all attempts to capture the position failed, owing to the steady and deliberate fire of the 57th and 16th who were, moreover, running short of ammunition.

How then would these masses have fared in the face of the modern breech-loader ?

The liability of massed formations to become disorganized.

Let us watch them now as they advance. They must necessarily be continually closing and opening out, their shape and size continually altering, and hopelessly obstructing the full development of fire and movement. Surely this alone will convince us as to the impracticability of such a system.

Our great object is to bring the whole moral and physical strength of each individual man to bear, and make the most of every single rifle. Let strategy alone be responsible for the employment of "masses" at the right time and place.

One of the greatest factors in an action, is good shooting. These "masses" come into action so exhausted and excited that it is a physical impossibility for them to fire carefully, and the same thing happens when doubling up before re-opening fire. The double is indeed our greatest enemy, for it practically disarms our Infantry. In proof of this I need only instance our manœuvres. Yet, without good firing, no attack can possibly succeed. It merely means waste of ammunition, and that, too, without any adequate means of replenishing the supply.

The "Double" a great mistake in the attack.

Let us assume that the position occupied by the defenders is a good one, the ground favourable and that their heads only are visible. The assailants, we will suppose, have advanced to within 800 mètres (900 yards) of the position, which is about the limit under modern conditions of fire.

The uselessness of long range fire on prepared positions.

Fire must now be opened, and that too under a continuous fire from the defenders. It is difficult enough even at manœuvres to distinguish men well placed at 900 yards, and although officers may do so with glasses, we cannot give every man a field glass, nor, if we did, could they shoot with them! The defenders are therefore firing with all the advantages, which are absolutely denied to the assailants! Does any one really imagine that "skirmisher masses" after advancing from 2,000 to 800 or 700 mètres under fire, and part of that distance at the double, can possibly silence the fire of the defenders? It is certainly done at manœuvres, but then, as I said before, it is unfortunately quite a different matter in the battle-field.

Even assuming that by "mass Tactics" we mean numerical superiority on an equal frontage, I cannot admit the possibility of success. Having reached the most effective zone, these "masses" must be at a disadvantage, and having failed to subdue the enemy's fire they cannot advance one single step further, and thus the battle is ended, just as it was at St. Privat. The very best officers in the world cannot save the day. It is stated in the History of the "Queen's" Regiment* that the only thing that saved it from annihilation was the fact that the enemy fired too high. Although, of course, this might happen again, we must never rely on it.

---

* German "Regiment Konigin."

Moral effect cannot be developed with massed formations.

The actual moral force in a massed body of skirmishers is very small, especially in regard to fire effect, while their casualties must be very numerous, and failing sufficient impulse from the rear, the moral effect of the enemy's fire must check the advance. Both the strong and weak side of human nature must be considered; the instinct of self-preservation exists in every human being. Like every other "science," Tactics must be steadily improved and developed on sound principles. What improvement, I would ask, are "mass Tactics" on those of Frederick the Great? Yet we are asked to believe that a disorganized mass, the greater portion of which can never fire; and must stand there helpless to be shot down, can silence the enemy's fire. By substituting "massed skirmishers" for "massed columns," we have gone from one extreme to the other. The word "mass" is an ominous one, and should be erased from our tactical dictionary. It is not until the assailants reach the decisive distance that numbers begin to tell, and the assailants find themselves on equal terms with the enemy as regards fire effect. This distance is about 400 yards. It is therefore here that the assailants gain the moral effect so indispensible to success. Not only must this distance be reached at all hazards, but it must be reached with the men standing shoulder-to-shoulder in one long firing line so as to deliver the most effective massed fire. The line, moreover, must be composed of fresh troops and not of shattered and exhausted fragments devoid of energy. Then and then alone must the tide turn. No Reserves can then help the defenders. They will lose confidence in their weapons, and stagger before the terrific close range fire of the attack. Confusion, excitement, and panic

Importance of having fresh troops at the final stage.

must follow, firing becomes wild and hurried, and their condition being thus betrayed, let the flood-gates of the assault be now opened, let the "masses" be hurled in, for this is the one and only supreme moment, when to economize them would be wrong. All casualties must be ignored, if victory is to be secured. In future the attack must be prepared to suffer heavily; but it must be led with all the greater intelligence. The amount of resistance depends of course on the fire and discipline of the defenders, but beyond that, it becomes merely a question of moral stamina on which we cannot speculate.

Yet there is every reason why we should make a close study of the probable conditions of future warfare. We must expect the "defence" to accomplish as much as the "attack." We must be prepared to meet an enemy, who will hold out till the very last, who is striving to attain a victory unparalleled in the annals of military history, and who, when he has fired his last cartridge, will use his bayonet and fight for victory to the death. Such is the "defence" we shall be asked to "attack" and crush.

And now let us see whether this commonly accepted theory of the immense difficulties of an attack is true or not. What is the "attack"? One of the factors of the battle. What is the "defence"? The other factor of the battle. What is the "battle"? The product of two equal factors, "attack" and "defence." Or, are these factors unequal to start with? Certainly not, if we are to believe military history. When pike fought pike, the "attack" certainly succeeded as often as the "defence," therefore surely it must be the same when breech-loader fights

Meaning of "Attack" and "Defence."

breech-loader. What constitutes the superiority or inferiority of the "attack" to the "defence"? Superior or inferior arms. But at the present time, both are equally well armed. Under normal conditions "attack," and "defence" must be equal, and although Clausewitz, undoubtedly a military expert of the first order, has spoken so much in favour of the "defence," I venture to hold to my opinion that, given equally good weapons, there is nothing more in favour of the one than the other. The "attack" is neither easier nor more difficult than it used to be. Its difficulties have increased only in proportion to those of the defence. The only condition that has changed is that of "range," and even that affects both sides to the same extent. As regards the defence, I think we may fairly assume that the "task" has certainly been rendered no easier. The selection of a position, employment of Reserves, etc., etc., are all far more difficult than they used to be. Modern weapons have rendered the conduct of the fight more difficult for both and the whole question resolves itself into one of the capacity of the commander. When we have brought the attack up to the final zone and have silenced the enemy's terrible massed fire, what will happen? The old hand-to-hand fighting must now be fought out with the rifle, not the bayonet. The former physical impetus given to the assailants at close quarters is now replaced by the great moral factor of fire effect, and herein lies the secret of silencing the fire of the defenders. To be successful, "fire and movement" must be so closely connected and strongly combined that the one is dependent upon the other.

Summary of the problems of the modern Infantry attack.

The problems of the Infantry "attack," under modern conditions, may therefore be summed up somewhat in the following manner:—

(1) How to bring the most effective possible fire to bear upon the defenders at the closest possible range?

(2) The best means of preventing disorganization and keeping units intact?

(3) How to maintain the influence of commanders throughout each stage of the fight?

(4) How to ensure larger units (up to at least a brigade) working together and delivering a simultaneous attack?

(5) How to avoid the waste of ammunition, and ensure the replenishment of it under all circumstances?

CHAPTER III.

"EXTENDED ORDER" is the only practical method adapted to modern warfare; it has been necessitated by the destructive and searching power of modern breech-loading rifles, and by all the natural laws of tactics, we must give this extended order some definite tactical organization. Thence we have three primary conditions to fulfil, and these are:—

"Extended order" must be tactically organized.

(1) The utmost development of force.

(2) Reduction of casualties to a minimum.

(3) Continuity of organization and control.

With the modern rifle, it is as if we had an explosive force to deal with. We must minimize its bursting powers by clearing the space around it, before we can proceed to work satisfactorily. Our motto must be "Confidence combined with control." We Infantry men imagine we have made extraordinary progress in the art of war, and believe that we have solved the problems of modern warfare. What then are these problems? and why should the attack be more impossible than the defence? I think we must start by realizing the fact that the present system is a diseased one, and that what we call the problems of the attack are merely the symptoms of a malignant disease. The two most obvious chronic symptoms are the "double

Present system diseased and out of date.

company column" and "skirmisher swarm." The system, feeling its own weakness, has taken refuge in that so-called remedy, "cover," which, more especially since the introduction of the breech-loader, has tied us hand and foot. How are we then to escape from these fetters, and work once more on sound principles? Self-help is the only remedy. Then the symptoms will disappear, then we shall lop off the last heads of the dreaded Hydra, Shrapnel and breech-loaders, then we shall have cleared the way for intelligent and energetic action, the only road to victory. Owing to the many ramifications of an action, the friction between higher and subordinate commanders is unavoidable; the only question is whether this is to be regarded as a fault or symptom of weakness. Faults are due to human nature, while symptoms of weakness are organic, and the system is responsible for them. Subordinate commanders must always be present where their superiors can never be. The commander of an army corps could never supervise the work of a battalion or company. His task ends with the evolution of his scheme, the details of which his officers must carry out. If the scheme is adapted to the requirements of modern armament, in every possible way, then the relations between commanders and subordinates will also be satisfactory. In nature, just as in our everyday life, there are certain forces that cannot be controlled by mere brute force, but only by prudence; and modern rifles are just such a "vis major." The failure of Napoleon's masses at "La Belle Alliance," and the Russian "masses" at Plevna, were due, not so much to the English or Turkish fire, as to the foolish attempts to break troops in "extended order."

As regards "cover" we find that it is liable to be just as dangerous as it is helpful. By resorting unconditionally to cover, the tactical organization of units is so disturbed that, as a rule, hopeless confusion is the result. Of course there are most cogent psychological reasons for this tendency to seek cover; but the adoption of massed formations assists this tendency to no small extent. The rapidity with which troops discern "cover" is marvellous. It seems to magnetically attract them, and if, as is generally the case, those to either flank also discover it, we find one spot occupied by two or three compact bodies instead of one. Indeed military history contains many instances of this having been done. Supposing, for instance, that the cover in question is in the form of a semicircle towards the enemy's position. We may be fairly certain that every company will occupy it, and, it need scarcely be pointed out, the line of fire having been broken, and fire effect thus reduced to a minimum, what a splendid opportunity it affords the enemy to deliver a flank attack. It has been truly observed that any units acting thus in real warfare would court destruction. Yet the advance must be made, and what then? Either annihilation, or the absence of any proper tactical formation in which to advance, and hence our dilemma!

Cover subordinate to tactics.

Under the present system with its natural tendency to disintegration, commanders must necessarily lose touch with their troops, and, in proportion to their loss of control, so subordinate commanders must be given independence and freedom of action. Military history teaches us that one of the features of all recent battles has been the issue of hurried and confused orders, often resulting in rash and foolish actions. This occurred in 1870-71 in both the French and German armies. It has been ascribed to the appalling effect of fire when suddenly opened, and it is said that it is far more likely to occur with the destructive power of the new rifle. Yet, it is intrinsically the same whether we wage war with "pikes" or with "breech-loaders." War is, and must ever remain, the greatest sphere of danger; all the physical and moral forces of man are put to the utmost possible tension; decisions must be made and orders given very rapidly, and carried out on the instant. It does not however follow naturally that war must mean hurry, confusion, indecision or incompetence. Such are the symptoms of the present system in its diseased condition, and the relief of these symptoms we must take as the 7th problem of the Infantry Attack of the present day. Each act in the great drama of war must be intelligently and carefully opened, gathering force as it progresses and finally crushing and carrying all before it like an avalanche. If we give "extended order" some concrete tactical organization, then we secure that element of imposing calm so sure a proof of a good drama, and we may surely claim for war the title of the best, most powerful, and most realistic drama in life. True, the system has altered the supports formerly in rear of the fighting line have been pushed up from the commencement, but the formations themselves are still the same.

Immense difficulties of Cavalry reconnaissance.

The mistakes and confusion which have marked so many recent battles, have not seldom been ascribed to insufficient reconnaissance by Cavalry. Every action, it is stated, should be preceded by a most careful and searching reconnaissance by Cavalry, and on this all plans should be evolved. Yet how, I would ask, would a Cavalry reconnaissance have affected the Russian plan of attack at Plevna, and what results would they have achieved with smokeless powder? Are we not unconsciously reminded of the words

> "Die Botschaft hör ich wohl
> Allein mir fehlt der Glaube."

"I hear the message, but have not faith."

With modern rifles Cavalry cannot reconnoitre Infantry positions sufficiently to admit of plans being evolved, unless the defenders have neglected every ordinary precaution. There are, in the first place, two sides to the question. One force desires to make a reconnaissance whilst the opposing one uses every possible means of frustrating it, the result being that any extended reconnaissance is impossible without a collision. Now that smokeless powder is used, Cavalry patrols may often be shot down without knowing whence the firing comes.

Cavalry may indeed congratulate themselves if they can give roughly the extent of the position occupied, and yet it is the commonest fallacy of the present day to suppose that they can make a complete reconnaissance of a position occupied by the enemy's Infantry. I do not mean that Cavalry are to blame in any way. They are and must ever be, the eyes of an army, and we may rest assured that they will achieve as gallant deeds in the future as they have done in the past. Then again we must remember that in the matter of reconnaissance, the defenders have the advantage. . Having a fixed and definite plan of defence, they can adapt their reconnaissance accordingly, whilst the elements of chance must affect the assailants, and under such conditions there is not much doubt as to where the greatest probability of success lies. An advancing enemy (*i.e.*, the assailant,) is far easier to discover than the defenders of a position, even if balloons be employed. Moreover, our manœuvres teach us that it is purely illusory to imagine that any plan of attack can be formulated on the results of a Cavalry reconnaissance.

Who then is to discover the enemy's position and strength? The attacking Infantry, and they alone. In future warfare, the first thing to be done will be to feel the enemy, that is, to get touch with him and force him to betray his dispositions. We may therefore take it as imperative for Infantry to maintain the so-called "demonstrative" as long as possible before adopting the "offensive," more particularly when attacking prepared positions. I propose later on to deal with this "demonstrative" phase more in detail.

CHAPTER IV.

Probable nature and duration of future campaigns and battles.

WARS will in future probably be of short duration, but battles will last longer. The armies that meet will be of such size as has never been conceived. Each will enter the field with the same primary object, and it will be to the interest of each to employ the whole available force at once, for there will be but little chance of recovery after the first decisive blow. No theory based on past experience can give us any idea of the tenacity and obstinacy with which these armies will fight. Moreover, we must be prepared to find that our own particular adversary is as efficient as we think ourselves to be. Without this we can never hope for ultimate success.

How to study military history.

Military history is undeniably an inexhaustible treasury wherefrom to glean all our tactical knowledge, but it must be studied with an unbiased and impartial mind. We must search as deep as possible to find the cause of all errors committed, with a view of rendering their recurrence impossible. Attacks such as were delivered at Plevna should certainly never have been made, and yet we often hear these very errors raised to the actual level of tactical precepts. In his day, Griesheim was held up as a great authority on Tactics, but latterly his theories were proved to be seriously at fault. And after all this was but natural, since they were based on the errors committed during the War of Independence.

Progress actually made in Tactics during the present century.

Our present "system" of attack will alone shew how very little progress we have made during this present century, the reason being our great tendency to take the last war as a perfect model, in spite of the introduction of new weapons. We assume that everything must happen just as it did in the last campaign, never troubling to enquire why errors were committed, or wherein they lay. All our efforts towards improvement have been at best half-hearted, and half-hearted measures are worse than useless, for they lead to doubt and vacillation. Before all things the art of war requires to be intelligently handled. If to become a great strategist merely meant a study of strategy, then indeed the task would be simple. When "von Moltké" made his flank march to the north, and fought with his front reversed at Metz, he certainly disobeyed all rules and principles of strategy; yet his action was justified, because he had thought out carefully exactly what he *intended* to do, and knew exactly what he *could* do. Indeed, there are many episodes in the 1870-71 war, which could not be submitted to a strict tactical examination, but for which Moltké was in no way to blame.

Errors committed in 1870-71 due to force of political circumstances.

In those days Tactics did not occupy such a prominent position as a science, and by far the most of the errors committed were due to political circumstances. When these brooked no delay whatever in preparing for war, tactics were bound to suffer, and the result was a more or less hybrid system. It may therefore be some consolation to us to know that in 1870-71 it was not our "Tactics," but our pre-eminent "Strategy" that led to victory. In future, however, tactics will play a far more important, if not decisive part. Strategy will have a freer hand, in proportion as "Tactics" (by which I mean the direction and control of troops throughout the fight) can be relied upon, and the same relation will exist between "Tactics" and actual fighting.

Political objects subordinate to strategy.

The only possible strategical objective is the main body of the hostile army, until that is vanquished, the political object cannot be attained. To attain the latter, not only genius and ability are required, but the subjection of the enemy's forces, and therefore fighting. The best strategy in the world will avail nothing without really efficient troops, and yet although the "fight" itself is the inevitable basis of all tactical and strategical combinations, its method is studied less than anything else; in all our studies of military history vast attention is paid to "Tactics" and "Strategy" while the actual details of the "fight" are omitted as unworthy of consideration. If an action is unsuccessful, we attribute it to the incapacity of individual commanders, whereas this is by no means the rule. Take, for instance, a description of an Infantry engagement such as is only too often to be found in recent military history :—

"The advance-guard meets the enemy. The battalion in front deploys for attack, and succeeds in capturing the enemy's position. The men are, however, completely exhausted, companies are broken up and mixed, and there is general confusion. While company commanders are engaged in reorganizing their companies, the enemy makes a vigorous counter-attack, the result being that the battalion is forced to act on the 'defensive' in a disorganized condition. Recognizing the gravity of the situation, the regiment sends up reinforcements and every possible endeavour is made to save the situation. The dense 'skirmisher swarms,' having had to advance at the double, arrive breathless and decimated by the enemy's fire. In their eagerness to advance companies are again mixed up, it is impossible to make any orders heard, and the regiment is driven back by the enemy's fire, in a totally disorganized condition. The Brigadier then collects the remnants, and advances with the 2nd regiment. Placing himself at the head of his troops, he carries all before him by his personal courage and example, *but*——he fails to recapture the position. The brigade with its skirmisher masses suffers severely from the enemy's fire, tactical units are broken up, all attempts at reorganization failing in the excitement and confusion of the moment. The brigade then finally retires a dense huddled mass, in which the enemy's bullets cleave great gaps."

As to the reason of these disastrous results, it is stated "that it is merely the natural consequence of modern rifle fire. Infantry engagements *must* always end thus, *but*," it is resumed, "it was leadership that failed. Had one commander not neglected to do this, and another given such and such orders, the result would have been very different." Leadership, where "swarms" or "masses" are concerned, is perhaps almost an impossibility. It is the dense and unwieldy form of our "columns" and "swarms" that renders men so powerless and helpless, and prevents them from exerting their physical and moral forces to the utmost.

Element of danger increased.

The zone of danger has now been enormously increased. Safety is almost out of the question at any distance, and when in danger, men demand free scope for their strength and will, and instinctively desire to be as little exposed as possible. Now neither the "double rank" nor "swarm formation" meet any of these requirements, with the result that the men lose confidence in their leaders, and are apt to become demoralized. When forming these "skirmisher masses," each man is free to go in front or behind as he likes, and therefore on purely psychological grounds both "swarms" and "masses" should be abandoned. Human nature being, as a rule, weak, it behoves us to consider its weak and not its strong side. By the terms of general conscription now obtaining in all continental Armies, every man is forced to serve who is physically fit, and yet the period of service is too short to admit of the soldier developing the best soldierly qualities. Nature certainly comes to our rescue in the hour of danger; courage, strength, and self-reliance are often engendered by danger, but only when a man has a means of defence, and the full and free use of those means. A tactical system must therefore be based on psychological principles, for with the appalling effect of modern rifle-fire, these can least be dispensed with.

How to minimize it.

Examination of present systems.

We will now proceed to examine the formations at present used by most armies, *viz.*, the "double-rank company column" and "skirmisher swarm."

One section extends, the 2nd section prolongs, and eventually the 3rd or 4th sections complete the extension. Thus we have a company divided into 3 or 4 new subordinate units, formed in the middle of the fight, and thus must the company remain until the end. With such a tactical organization, control and supervision both when firing and advancing, are, I maintain, almost impossible. The company cannot develop its whole force, and while extending the losses may be so heavy as to end the battle before the advance is resumed. When once the company has advanced, it has lost all its elasticity; it is not tactically self-contained, and therefore cannot adapt itself to the variable conditions of the fight. Fresh "swarms" are now pushed up, the final result being that units are hopelessly mixed up. History tells us that that was what happened, and in future these errors will occur far more frequently.

Let us now assume that the Infantry of an Army corps is advancing to attack. Each division receives its orders, and the plan of attack is distributed to each unit, down to the battalion or even the company. Everything being then as it were cut and dried, and each commander carrying out the portion of the scheme allotted to him, the Army corps has fulfilled its object. Such is theory. Now let us see how it is in practice. What happens, for instance, while the corps is getting into position? Endless difficulty and confusion, and as soon as the attack is commenced, these are intensified so as to leave us ultimately a veritable "parody on tactics." It then merely depends upon whether the enemy seizes his opportunity; if he be only moderately capable, the issue of the fight must hang in the balance. What we then have to do, is to evolve a scheme by which a complete Army corps may deliver an attack, and having already dismissed the question of a "normal" system as most dangerous, we must seek elsewhere for our primary basis. In the first place, we must develop the technicalities of fighting to the utmost extent in the fighting unit, *i.e.*, the company, before we can succeed with larger bodies ; and although these technicalties must of course in a way be of a normal nature, they must be aselastic and adaptable to ground and surrounding circumstances as possible. "But," it may be argued, "the 'swarm' system answers all these requirements, and the Germans won all their battles in 1870, fighting on this system": I would then ask, how it was that the French *lost* every battle ,adopting precisely the same formations ?

Summing up we find then that the main defects of the "swarm" system are as follows :—

Defects of the present system.

1. The fighting efficiency of each individual man, which is the only guarantee of success for the whole unit, is not maintained with sufficient continuity.

2. The frontal strength of the company is tactically far too small, and is consequently liable as a rule to be reduced to a minimum just when the hardest fighting commences.

3. By making companies and sections tactically independent, commanders lose control throughout the battle and confusion is inevitable.

4. Units must pass through one another and get mixed up when under fire.

The following are the chief points therefore to which we should turn our attention :—

Main objects to be attained in evolving a system.

(*a*) Train the individual soldier and develop his fighting instinct as much as possible. Victory will not depend upon numbers alone, but the system in which they are employed.

(*b*) The strength of the company must be self-contained, so that it may carry home the attack without support of any kind.

(*c*) The company must be raised to the status of the one and only fighting unit.

(*d*) All possibility of units finding themselves without commanders during an action must be eliminated.

As the company is the fighting unit, so the battalion is the tactical unit, and therefore no one below a battalion commander should *direct* the fight.

Fire effect under the present system.

As regards fire effect, bodies of Infantary commence firing at 1,000 mètres, and fire is effective against company columns at 1,200, and massed battalions at 1,500 mètres. A clear field of vision, knowledge of range, and steady aim being indispensible to good firing, we find that, between 1,000 and 600 mètres, the fire of the defenders must be so far superior to that of the assailants, that the latter could never exchange shots without suffering heavily. "Swarms" advancing between these distances, shoulder to shoulder, would lose enormously. What then are the assailants to do, since they cannot fire, and cannot advance without heavy loss? Are we to push up still more "swarms" so as to make sure of some "fragments" at least reaching the final zone? Scarcely so, if we recognize the effect of modern breech-loaders. Such rifle fire is an insatiable monster whose motto is "the more the better" and these "fragments" will make but little or no impression upon the defence. No, this massed fire of the defence must be combated by ingenuity, in other words, we must present the smallest possible target.

How to ensure an advance up to the closest range with a minimum loss.

At any thing over 350 mètres, it is impossible to aim at *single objects*. Thus the logical conclusion is that our "attack" formation should be such as to present *single objects*, and thus admit of an advance up to within 350 mètres of the enemy, with the minimum loss. Such a method being based on scientific and logical principles should become an immutable law, though, of course, like everything earthly, the element of chance has to be considered and therefore some casualties must occur. If, on the other hand, we employ "massed bodies" we merely carry out exactly what the defenders require, and then our casualties are no longer due to chance, but are a natural consequence. Now we come to the crucial point of the whole fight. Within 350 mètres, our casualties are no longer accidental, and it is at this point therefore that the great musketry duel must be fought out in future battles, and it is on the issue of this duel, that the fate of the attack will depend. From 1,000 mètres onwards, the only practical or possible system must be one of "extended lines" with large intervals, for against these the defenders' fire will have the least effect. After reaching 600 mètres, the assailants' fire commences to neutralise the advantage hitherto held by the defence, until at 350 mètres it gains the upper hand. If the

The limits of "chance" and "aimed" casualties.

assailant can reach this final zone without halting, and therefore without firing, he should make the very most of this advantage. If, however, fire has to be opened *before* reaching this zone, there remains nothing but the best possible combination of " fire and movement."

The theory for the attack which I would propose is therefore based on the following principles :—

Principles on which a future attack should be based.

(1) Every possible endeavour to be made to reach the final zone without halting.

(2) Failing this an advance up to 600 mètres, which ought to be possible with skilful leading.

(3) From 600 mètres up to the final zone (350 mètres), combination of "fire with movement."

(4) Up to the final zone, the formation to be in single rank " *extended.*"

(5) After reaching the final zone, the line to be as strong as possible, the men shoulder to shoulder, so as to obtain the utmost possible fire effect. All casualties to be replaced at once, and every single available rifle brought to bear on the enemy's position, the defenders thus losing their material advantage, whilst the attack gains that great essential point, " moral effect."

Human nature being impossible to guage under every possible condition, it is impossible to provide for cases where positions are held to the very last. The distance at which fire effect will be decisive must depend upon circumstances, and cannot be fixed as a hard and fast rule. In general, however, we shall find that we must in these matters inevitably bow to the natural laws of science on which my theory is based. We may take it for granted that the assailants' fire will be effective at 600 mètres, and if massed might possibly dislodge the defenders. How very much sooner then would success be attained, if this massed fire were brought to bear on the enemy at 350 mètres?

The best system of adapting "extended order."

The penetrative power of modern rifles is the most cogent reason possible for avoiding double rank formations, but, as we have already seen, a single rank formation shoulder to shoulder resolves itself into nothing less than a wall of human beings to catch the enemy's bullets. What therefore is the alternative? Nothing but what I have already advocated, *viz*:—"A dotted line with big intervals." The only question is how to stiffen these lines, and how to form our supports and reserves? The latter must be close at hand and available at short notice. Double or single rank column formations being as impracticable here as they are in the firing line, there is no alternative but still further open lines. These lines must not, however, cover the intervals in the firs tline, as then we should reconstruct our wall.

1st line
2nd line

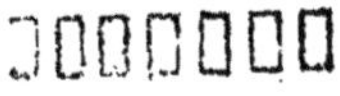

Incorrect.
Irregular but unbroken.

1st line
2nd line

Correct.
Regular but broken.

They must be placed as above, each line exactly covering the other at say 20-30 mètres distance. Simultaneous casualties will seldom occur, for as a rule a bullet will turn and pass through the intervals of the second line. Direct casualties in the second line are of course possible. Indeed heavy casualties are possible with such an open formation, but even so I maintain that it is the only one which admits of getting within striking distance of the defence.

The first line must engage the enemy lying down, thus drawing and depressing their fire, by which means the lines in rear will be enabled to advance.

To deliver a successful attack, we must not mass our troops in rear, and spread them out to the front, we must have them *extended* and *loosely formed* in rear, and *concentrated* as they approach the enemy thus:—

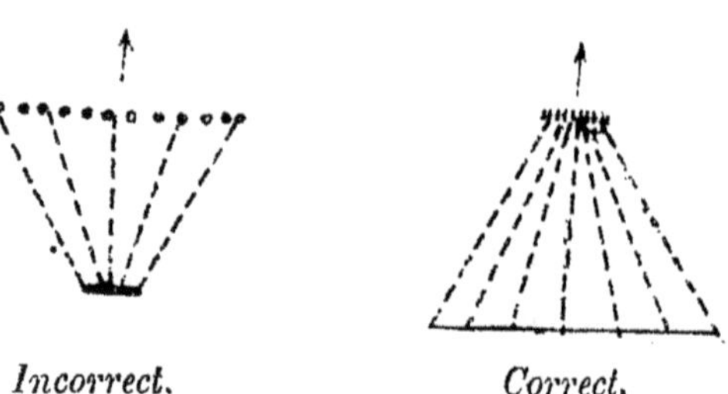

Incorrect. *Correct.*

Let us now see what is understood by our *present* system of "extended order." It is certainly something in the nature of a "contradiction in terms," for the term "extended" or "scattered"* is opposed to the idea of "order," and "tactics," as its name implies, is the "art of

* The German word is "Zerstreute" which literally means "scattered" or "spread."

"Extended order" as understood under our present system.

order." Extended order (or *scattered* order) is therefore so closely allied to "*Dis*order" that it cannot be reasonably included under the term "Tactics," and there seems to have been great difficulty in christening this tactical malformation at its very birth. "Open order" did not sound well, while "extended order" did not imply "order." "Loose order" was a direct contradiction in terms, for if "order" is "loosened" it ceases to exist. The result of all this was a feverish desire to obtain preponderance of fire at the very commencement at all hazards, and at a range too where the fire of the attack must necessarily be far inferior to that of the defence. If, instead of adopting what we call "extended order" as a last resource, our "column formation" had been made more elastic, we should have obtained the utmost possible fire effect, the men would have been kept well in hand, and the present "*problems of the attack*" would never have existed.

CHAPTER V.

Definite proposals for a new "attack formation."

IN formulating the following proposals for organizing an attack formation to meet the requirements of modern weapons, I must first state that I do not lay any claim to perfection. In a paper of this nature I am of course precluded from working out minor details. As long as the company commander is given sufficient freedom of action, the actual conduct of the fight rests with him. How he is toemploy the means at his disposal, whether he is to extend his company gradually, and other numerous details, must be left entirely to his intelligence, common sense, and power of adapting his mode of action to circumstances, for any hard-and-fast "sealed pattern" must of necessity cripple his intelligence, and be attended with the most disastrous results in the field.

Introductory remarks.

The formation I propose for adoption is one of "columns," as being most suitable for keeping troops well in hand, and the most likely to ensure success. These columns are, however, not to be formed with the object of assaulting with the bayonet, *i.e.*, the great object aimed at, is to obtain the best possible fire effect from every available rifle. "Columns" can, moreover, be better adapted to the configuration of the ground than "swarms" or "masses"; they neither conform to the principles of "extended" or "close" order, but they are conducive to the most efficient "fighting order," and are at the same time least liable to be affected by the enemy's fire. Orders are prevented from miscarrying, and units maintain their integrity, while the system is equally well adapted to either the "offensive" or "defensive."

A company is assumed to be at war strength (*i.e.*, 200 men).

*(i) Company Column.**

"Company column."

This will be formed 4-deep with 25 paces between each line (or rank), as this distance corresponds to the frontal breadth of half a line. (See plate I.) †

(ii) Skirmishing Column.‡

"Skirmishing column."

Each rank now extends to 3 paces from the centre, the distance between ranks (or lines) being increased to 50 paces. (See plate I.)

(iii) Attacking Column. §

"Attacking column."

The distance between the ranks is now increased to 100 or 200 mètres. This is merely taken for purposes of illustration. Of course the distance would vary according to the nature of the ground and other circumstances. It may, for instance, be found advisable to maintain the "skirmishing column" formation, with the first line *only* pushed several hundred mètres forward.

(iv) Column of March. ‖

Each line of "company column" forms "files" from the centre towards each flank. To assume "column of march" formation, these files close on the centre from left and right, so as to form "double files" (of 4 men each). "Company column" is *re*formed by the files coming up on the left and right.

---

* German "Kompagnie kolonne."

† All these formations are far more simple on the plan proposed ("section column." See Appendix.)

‡ German "Schutzen kolonne."

§ German "Angriff's kolonne."

‖ The German is "Marsch kolonne." This seems an unnecessarily round about way of assuming the desired formation. It would be simpler to close on the centre (of each line), and then form fours. See Appendix.—*(Translator.)*

"Column of march."

It is not necessary to form the whole column simultaneously, *e.g.*, any of the above formations may have their first "line" some 100 mètres ahead formed as in skirmishing column.

Each formation can be adopted from any other as desired. The company can form line for massed fire from either of these four formations, and revert to any formation from line.

To close the whole company, the lines merely have to march to the front or rear and close on the centre simultaneously. *

By fixing the interval at 3 paces for manœuvres, the three rear lines will find ample room to fire in any position when they have joined the firing line, and tactical units will be almost as large as if they were at war strength.

Importance of representing casualties during manœuvres.

In my opinion it is most important, not only for tactical but for psychological reasons, that casualties should be adequately represented during peace-manœuvres. Men should be accustomed to the sight of dead and wounded lying about in all directions, and be stimulated with that noblest of all desires, to conquer or die for their fatherland. We should reduce a soldier's first impressions in the field as much as possible, by preparing him for them during peace time.

Assuming that the casualties amount to one quarter, which amount would be distributed over the four ranks (or lines), we may fix the interval at 2 paces, giving the company a frontage of 120

---

* The author's system is best likened to a "concertina." —*(Translator.)*

mètres,* which is practically identical with that laid down in the German Drill Regulations.

(v) *Close Company Column.*†

I have shewn that the company can close on the centre from any of these formations, and this formation we will call "close company column." It will be found most convenient when taking cover or marching up into position when the large intervals and distances are not required.

Position of officers and non-commissioned officers.

The positions of officers commanding these lines, would be 4 paces in front of the centre. The company commander, being alone responsible for his company in action, must select his position. When the company is closed and in single rank, he should, of course, be in the centre, so as to ensure the correct transmission of orders. His officers and non-commissioned officers should be at his disposal in front.

Thus we have each line forming a "fire group" under an officer, and, when in single rank, a "fire group" under the company commander.

The attack would be carried out somewhat on the following lines:—

Method of carrying out the attack.

1. The "skirmishing column" having reached the extreme limit of the "demonstrative stage," or, let us say, 1,000 mètres from the enemy's position, and the attack having been decided upon, "attacking column" is formed to the front. The first line will, if possible, advance to 350

---

* Presumably after all the lines have joined the front line. The author's meaning is somewhat obscure; and it is not clear how he arrives at these 120 mètres, unless he presumes that the lines close on the centre on the occurrence of casualties. This is however a matter of detail. But see Appendix page 79.—*(Translator.)*

† German, "Geschlossene kompagnie kolonne."

mètres, or the decisive range, when it will halt, lie down, and open fire. Under cover of this fire the other lines will be brought up, until the company is formed in single rank, when massed fire is opened, every single effective rifle being thus brought to bear upon the enemy.

Supports and Reserves. Sometimes, of course, whole companies must be kept in support or reserve. If the first company fails, and its casualties are very heavy, the reserve company must send up as many lines as required, and eventually renew the assault. This will in no way disturb continuity of command, for the senior officer in the firing line will take command. It does not signify to the men, for they know that all orders must emanate from the centre, while the formation of new "command units" is avoided.

When to open fire. 2. Fire should on no account be opened up to 600 mètres. Should it be found absolutely necessary to open fire at this distance, the first line will halt, and commence firing, the remaining lines advancing *through* one another for about 100 mètres, lying down and firing alternately, until the fourth line becomes the first.

If it be desired to commence massed fire the rear (first) line advances and carries the front line with it, and so on, until the whole company is in single rank, the front line continuing the fire while this is being done.*

How to continue fire from one position. 3. Each line carries 7,500 rounds, with which a considerable amount of execution should be done by good shots, but if it be found necessary to continue firing by individual lines for a still further period, the lines in rear will remain lying down until the order is given to advance by one or more successive rushes.

4. If the first line is under fire at 600 mètres the other lines continue the advance, the second line joins the first, and carries it forward to a fresh position. The remaining lines then come up, join the firing line successively, and carry it forward until the final zone is reached.* The Reserve company is meanwhile continuing its advance, and must replace casualties so as to keep the firing line up to full strength. Its formation must depend upon circumstances, but as it is originally formed four-deep, "attacking column" can be formed if necessary.

How to take up successive positions.

5. The first line having opened fire at 600 mètres, and the rear lines having successively joined it, after having developed the full fire of the company, the men must now be called upon for the most supreme effort ever demanded from human nature, for in such close formation the casualties may be very numerous up to 350 mètres from the enemy. The first line must now rise, advance and seize a fresh position, the rear lines again closing up and joining it as already detailed, until the final zone is reached, thus giving the most effectual combination of fire and movement.

The above will perhaps suffice to shew roughly the outline of my scheme for an attack in deep formation.

---

* It is somewhat difficult to reconcile procedure in para. 4 with that of para. 2. What I think the author means is, that the advance of the lines through one another is only to be carried out if the advance is checked in any way, so as to keep up a certain degree of movement but that if it be desired to assume the decisive stage the rear lines come up and carry forward this first line to a new position, successively.—*(Translator.)*

The men are kept well in hand, reinforcement is tactically organized, units are kept intact, and the question of ammunition-supply, if not altogether solved, is at least within measurable distance of solution.

Concentric strength of system.

Everything depends upon the commander in the centre, and every man must therefore look straight ahead, there must be no "looking to the right or left for cover," although I do not mean to say that it should not be occupied, when it is met with in the right direction, and when it is advantageous to do so.

All changes of direction are most easily and safely made from the centre, even when made in conjunction with deployments.

All four formations are characterized by a natural tendency to secure a steady and concentric advance in the right direction, *i.e., the front.* The strength of the company lying in its centre, and not at its flanks, all movements are "wedge like" in their action. With our present system, when in "column of march," one flank is in front, and hence the difficulty experienced in advancing with the right front when attacking. The section is like a man who daren't look his adversary straight in the face, and therefore advances with his right shoulder up. Nor are we any better off with respect to the double-rank company column.

Receiving Cavalry in "company column."

In my system, the most powerful frontal development is ensured, while the company is enabled to act equally well to either flank or to the rear. Supposing, for instance, that the "company column" is attacked by Cavalry on the right flank. The orders would then be, "half lines—right form—quick march," giving a front of 110 rifles with which to receive Cavalry.

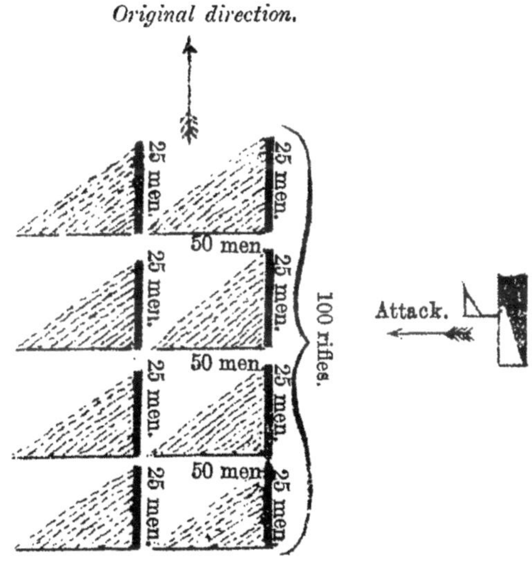

A. Company in "Company column" receiving Cavalry to the right.*

* The diagrams are made from the author's description.—(*Translator.*)

Receiving "swarms" or "masses" in "company column."

Or again, the left flank of the "skirmishing column" is attacked by "swarms" or "masses," when the orders would be:—"close to one pace interval—half lines, left form—march—right half lines reinforce," and we have 200 rifles at once in the firing line.

Original direction.

Attack.

200 rifles. After reinforcement of right half lines.

100 rifles.

25 men. 25 men. 25 men. 25 men. 25 men. 25 men. 25 men. 25 men.

50 50 50 50

25 men. men. 25 men. men. 25 men. men. 25 men. men

*A Company in * "Skirmishing column," receiving "swarms" or "masses."*

Applied to Artillery fire.

The system is equally well adapted to meet Artillery. If a "column of march" comes under Artillery fire, the order is merely given to "form skirmishing column." By adopting this formation men are given a feeling of safety at a time when they must be inclined to instinctively avoid danger. It minimizes the effect of Artillery fire, while the advance is neither retarded nor the direction altered.

---

* Diagrams made from author's description.—*(Translator.)*

Now let us see what happens under our present system.

The "attack" as developed under present system.

The head or point of the attack, being taken way from the head of the column, and therefore from a flank, engages the enemy; the line is formed by troops coming up on either flank or in the centre. The line is then tactically disorganized, and therefore tactically weak to start with, and the mere fact that so little cognizance is taken of this tactical weakness, is a proof that we have no really sound basis for our Infantry attack. Having satisfied ourselves that what we read in Military history must inevitably be repeated, we do not trouble to inquire into the reasons for these errors or evolve a system of avoiding them. Any new system is set down as a "dangerous experiment" and thus it is that our Infantry tactics are so out-of-date, that we are no longer in a position to take the field against modern weapons.

The one idea being to place a large number of rifles in the firing line, the extension is carried out by bringing up other sections, whereas it is moral effect alone that can secure the more material one of better fire. At anything over 350 mètres, the fire of the defence is so superior, that one company alone could practically annihilate a whole regiment, unless the latter were handled with the utmost skill. Moreover, it is inconceivable how such an extension could be carried out under fire owing to the lateral movements involved, and the fact of the second rank having to come up into line. The section remains massed for some considerable time, during which heavy losses must inevitably be incurred. We have

Heavy losses and delay inseparable from extensions to a flank.

only to see how these sections reach the firing line on a level parade-ground, and then imagine what would happen with a company at full strength in action, when the men would come up in driblets. We need only to send up the 3rd and 4th sections, and the picture is complete. All we have is a company "swarm," *i.e.*, a dense mass devoid of all tactical formation, and divided into 3 or 4 commands under section commanders, who must necessarily find it extremely difficult to keep touch, or work with their company commander. And yet this is the system on which we depend to "advance by rushes." Such a system may have been possible against muzzle-loaders, but its efficacy is more than doubtful against breech-loaders. It would be unreasonable to expect it of the average soldier, and it is undoubtedly these considerations that underlie the generally accepted theory that a frontal attack is no longer practicable.

Proposed system applied to one force engaging another acting on present system.

Let us now imagine a force, adopting my proposed system, engaged with an enemy adopting that of "skirmisher swarms." It is a "running fight," *i.e.*, neither side are in position. The heads of both columns are engaged at 600 mètres, and are 300 mètres distant from their nearest companies. We will assume that the ground is level and the attack purely frontal.

A company working on proposed system.

The company forms "skirmishing column," and is sent up to join the front "line," *i.e.*, to the head of the column to which it belongs. On the enemy's side we have No. 1 section, which moves out in "swarm" formation, and reinforces the head of the column, the other 2 or 3 sections forming company column and marching up in line.

We will assume that neither side opens fire, and that both companies when fully extended occupy the same frontage. I will now put the following questions:—

1. Which company will be able to open fire earliest and with most effect?

2. Which company has the best target to aim at?

3. Which company has most difficulty in extending, manœuvring, etc., and suffers most when so doing?

4. Which company is in the best position to assume the "offensive," and which has the most "defensive," power?

5. Which company holds the other inevitably at its mercy?

6. Which company can most rapidly develop its fullest fire effect?

7. Finally, in whose hands lies the power of assuming the initiative, and thus sealing the fate of the other?

These are the questions to which I would ask my readers to give their impartial consideration.

A battalion working on proposed system.

We will now take the case of a battalion working on my system, when I shall demonstrate where the line is to be drawn between tactical control and the actual conduct of the fight. The company forming the "advance-guard" of the battalion, on gaining touch with the enemy, forms "skirmishing column," and eventually "attacking column," either wholly or partially. The advance is then resumed until the first "line" is about 1,000 mètres from the enemy. A halt is then made, and a careful reconnaissance is carried out to the front and flanks of the enemy's position. The battalion commander then evolves his plans, which must be based on personal observation, information received, the object in view, nature of the ground, extent of the enemy's position, the strength of his force, &c., &c.

The attack is then commenced by companies. We will assume that four companies are extended alongside one another. These are then formed in "skirmishing columns." It will be found advisable to maintain an interval between companies of 25—30 paces.

It is at this point that "tactical control" must cease, the rest must now be left to the companies; we now change from the "demonstrative" to the "decisive" phase. Of course the battalion commander must still retain the power of tactical supervision. He must eventually settle how far the "attacking columns" are to advance at first, when to open fire, he must further see that the "decisive" or "final" assault is commenced simultaneously, *if necessary*. The depth of my formation enables all this to be satisfactorily accomplished, *if necessary*, but as a rule nothing more should be required when once the attack has been commenced.

This "demonstrative" phase, or, we will call it, the "preparative stage" is usually developed from 2,000 to 1,000 mètres from the enemy, and must be purely the work of the battalion commander or the Brigadier as the case may be. They must further be responsible for commencing the decisive stage at the right moment.

A brigade would act somewhat as follows :—

A brigade working on proposed system.

Two companies of each battalion in the first line.

Two companies of each battalion in the second line.

One battalion in rear of either flank or both battalions in rear of the centre, as a main Reserve.

Everything depends on the companies reaching the final zone together. The more carefully the "demonstrative" phase is developed, the greater the certainty of success. The secret of the "demonstrative" stage lies in orders reaching their destination simultaneously, whilst that of the attack, lies in simultaneous action by all units, from the smallest to the largest. Under the present system, there is no method whatever, by which the available strength is adapted to the required frontage, a point which I shall deal with in more detail later on.

CHAPTER VI.

WE will now consider the best means of protecting Infantry from Artillery fire, above and beyond their own means of self-defence.

Best means of protecting Infantry from Artillery fire.

In 1870-71, the German Artillery on several occasions practically decided the battle by their fire, whilst in future the effect of Artillery fire will exceed our expectations. Infantry losses may therefore be very heavy and the moral effect of Artillery fire may be most serious and far-reaching. Now, in all massed formations, including those at present in vogue, no provision whatever has been made to meet Artillery fire, with the result that if Infantry are suddenly exposed to it, some other formation must be adopted. This inevitably means hopeless confusion, and it is hardly necessary to point out how disastrous the effects will be, tactically because all organization ceases to exist, and morally, because the blunder being ascribed to commanders, the confidence of men is shaken.

Existing system as affected by Artillery fire.

Take for instance a battalion suddenly exposed to heavy Artillery fire, in "double rank column formation." "Extended company columns" must be at once formed. Even then the effect of Shrapnel fire is most searching, and the following orders will be probably given :—"1st section half right," "2nd section half left," "march." The battalion still being formed in more or less compact bodies, the losses are still heavy. The battalion commander therefore orders the whole battalion "half right" or "half left." When on the march the case is even worse if possible.

Now let us take a battalion under a similar fire, acting on the proposed system. The battalion is formed in "column of march," the only compact formation which the system admits of.

Proposed system as affected by Artillery fire.

One word of command only is required to open out the whole battalion: "Form skirmishing column." This operation proceeds quite naturally and easily, while tactical organization is in no way disturbed, the troops gain, instead of lose faith, whilst the casualties are reduced to a minimum, and "column of march" can be just as easily and rapidly resumed.

Safety and simplicity of proposed system as applied to the "company."

I now propose to discuss how far our "fighting unit," *i. e.*, "the company," is equal to the task assigned to it, when acting on my system. I venture to assert in the first place, this system will be hard to beat in the matter of simplicity and safety, – points of considerable importance not only in the field but in practical training. It admits of the soldier being trained individually in a rational manner, and it is on individual training that an army must depend for its efficiency and success in a campaign. That my "skirmishing" and "attacking" columns will be enabled to advance for a considerable distance without firing, will, I think, also be admitted, as also that the company will be enabled to bring its most effective fire to bear at the final zone.

I would therefore claim for my system:—

Advantages claimed for proposed system.

(*a*) That the individual qualities of each man have the widest scope for development.

(*b*) That there is a wholesome and self-contained impetus to move forward, from start to finish.

(*c*) That the men are as it were focussed on their commander.

(*d*) That lying down or running away is rendered impossible, each line being controlled by the next one.

(*e*) That this moral pressure from rear to front, so essential a condition of victory, cannot be exercised with our present system, which has a natural tendency to decentralize. This decentralizing tendency is, moreover, responsible for all the difficulties now experienced by officers in leading and directing their units. The excellent instructions drawn up for subordinate commanders are useless because it is impossible to carry them out. The skirmisher "mass" opens and closes by fits and starts; to rectify the error, and correct distances, it is closed here, and extended there, with the result that it waves to and fro and has no means of escape from this "circulus vitiosus."

(*f*) By applying the term "fighting unit" to any company, the company commander is alone all-powerful. His will must be absolute; he must be the life, soul and breath of the company. No section commander can clash with him, as is the case at present.

"Quot Capita, tot sensus," must be our leading maxim in future, if we wish to preserve that tactical "*order*," so essential a factor in leading troops to victory.

Subordinate commanders are merely assistants, their commands are in no sense tactical ones. Taking the individual company as an integral portion of a large body, what is it? The 24th part of a brigade, or the 100th part of an army corps, in short a "*tactical atom.*" Why, therefore, split it up still further? In view of the many demands made of a section commander in the present day, the command of a section has become an absolute art. "Shall I? Will I? Dare I?" must be the thoughts that present themselves to him. Are we not asking too much? Are we not paralyzing his will and determination? Our present system is based on the tactical independence of section commanders. One section is placed on the flank and there is itself exposed to flanking fire; another section advances too far and thus upsets the company commander's plans. Or, again, one section opens, or another ceases fire at the wrong moment, and I think we shall find that this was of such common occurrence in the last campaign, that it must be ascribed to nothing less than an ill-advised system. In my proposed system, although "line" commanders are individually vested with more responsibility, they cannot disturb the tactical dispositions in any way, and I think therefore it will be admitted that the primary conditions for enabling a section commander to carry out his duties are more apparent, in mine, than in the existing, system.

Excessive responsibility of section commanders under present system.

With the proportions that general conscription has now reached, it stands to reason that our fighting material must deteriorate. As von Moltke said, "we have not as many riflemen as rifles." Might we not adopt this aphorism and say we have not as many "soldiers" as we have "men"?

Fighting material deteriorated with general conscription.

The shorter the period of service, the more necessary it becomes to mark out men of specially soldier-like qualities. These exist, though not in sufficient numbers. *They* must be in the front line, for *they* are Moltke's "marksmen." It is *they* who must wear the "Dowe" shield on their hearts. Their influence on the "average" soldier will be immense, and it is to *them* that we must trust to give the moral impulse to the troops behind them, in the final and crowning phase of the battle.

"Elasticity" of proposed system.

In my system the formations are extremely elastic. All the innate strength and character of human nature is roused, whilst the weaker vessels are as it were taken in tow, and carried forward. There is no crowding or cramping; each man has every chance of doing his level best in the interests of the whole, while under the present system about six men cover one mètre of frontage, of which, under the most favourable conditions, only two are in the Reserve. Clock-work regularity permeates the system. There is a steady forward pressure from start to finish, with the one and only fixed determination to annihilate the enemy and gain an indisputable victory. The frontal strength is so great that an enemy occupying an equal frontage must be well nigh powerless to resist, and in a future campaign, where large bodies are opposed, this frontal strength is of vital importance. It is the frontal attack that must decide the battle, and woe betide the commander who knows not how to utilize his large numbers in an adequate manner. Numerical superiority will always tell, both strategically and tactically, but if we condense these numbers we not only minimize the effect of our fire but the more troops we waste, the more we hamper

Frontal strength of primary importance.

strategy. Faith in skilful leadership is the best and surest guarantee of discipline, and success depends upon superior leadership. If it be meant, however, that it is with *the present system* that a frontal attack is impracticable, then I admit the truth of the axiom. Those who assert that by adopting a system of " extended " order, discipline is liable to suffer, are greatly mistaken. To ensure the maintenance of discipline, we must first of all guard against our men being rendered defenceless, as they are in the " swarm " or "mass" system. We must bring them into action in a formation so organized, that each individual soldier *can* and *must* defend himself. If it becomes necessary to remain under fire, without returning it, the formation must be such as will give the men implicit confidence in their leaders.

Stimulation of individual action.

Such individual and independent action as I have advocated, stimulates the individual feeling of animosity. Every man is confronted with the alternative, " Either my enemy or myself ?" The soldier must reason with himself " the more of the enemy I kill, the better my own chances of safety, " with the result that he aims carefully and fires effectively. Under the present system none of these conditions exist. The men are not imbued with that feeling of self-defence, or responsibility, and being therefore dependent on their neighbours, their individual action is minimized. Laggards will lag, and such men will fire hurriedly and badly. The evils of our " mass " and " swarm " system become more apparent in proportion as we apply it to large bodies. In my system there is no " massing " until the final stage, and even then men have free use of their rifles, whilst the "massing" is carried out under cover of the fire of the first line. Before the final zone is reached, the defenders have practically no target to aim at, whereas "swarms" present an excellent target at 1,000 mètres both as regards length and depth. The leading company giving the direction, there is roused a keen competition to reach the place of honour, which ensures simultaneous concentration at the final stage. Losses being minimized, the men gain heart, and learn to ignore the enemy's fire. A most effective check is placed on any inclination to cowardice. Each line and each man are mutually controlled, and nothing is so effective on the whole. A soldier fears any suggestion of cowardice more from a comrade than from an officer, and since self-interest or his very life may be at stake, a comrade will certainly never allow another to escape at his own expense. This fear of being branded as a coward, both in the field and at home, drives the weakest hearts to face the greatest peril. When we see our "swarms" advancing "by mobs" as they do on parade, we scarcely realize what would happen in real warfare. We imagine that our men will, of their own free will, move from a position of perfect safety to one of imminent peril, the most severe strain it is possible to give their nerves. When these "rushes" are being made, men must naturally push and crowd together, with the result that when they reach the next position, perhaps half of them have no room to fire. Units become hopelessly confused, and all is disorganized. Were such errors due to faulty leadership, they would have been removed long ere this. All preliminary measures essential to the attack of a prepared position, can, under my system, be carefully and deliberately thought

Moral control.

out. *Cover must be subordinate to tactical considerations*, and such a formation as I propose is well adapted to the observance of this maxim. Frontal strength is of vastly more importance than that to a flank, and in this respect the "swarm" system is incomparably weaker. My open "lines" may be objected to as possessing too little capacity of fire when opposed to the enemy's massed fire. The "swarm" is in no better case, for its losses must be heavier while unnecessary. My "line" can aim carefully and deliberately. The "swarm" cannot. In my "line," each man fires independently, whereas in the "swarm" the men must fire *en masse*, and we need only turn to our musketry returns to see which fire is the better of the two. My first line gives the frontage of the whole company from the very commencement. It forms the frame-work whence the whole company's fire will be brought to bear. The length of this frontage is, as I have already stated, 120 mètres, of which ¼ is allowed for casualties. If these are more the men will have more room, and if less, then one line can be kept all the longer in "Reserve." I am further of opinion that ample frontage is a matter of vital importance in all combined frontal attacks, inasmuch as, although the assailant may have successfully reconnoitred the enemy's front, very little can be known regarding his depth. For this reason also the main "Reserves" should be separated. "Tactics" as conducted at present make no provision for the ever-changing relations of "strength" to "space," with the result that the system lives as it were from hand to mouth. Let us imagine, for example, that an enemy is defending a position 1 kilomètre (1,093 yards) in length. The position of the flanks are known, but not the depth. A brigade has to attack this position, and the deploying frontage therefore required is 1 kilomètre. Now comes the question as to how strongly this frontal space is to be occupied. A company requires 120 mètres, a battalion (with 2 companies in the 2nd line) 240 mètres, and therefore 1 brigade (6 battalions) 1,440 mètres. With 4 battalions a brigade would therefore occupy a frontage of about 1 kilomètre (1,000 mètres) each company has one in reserve immediately in rear, and 2 battalions can (on my system only) follow in rear of the centre. This position they must maintain under any circumstances, until the situation has developed.

Comparison between frontage of existing and proposed systems.

I will ask my readers to work out a similar example on the "swarm" system, and I do not think there is much doubt as to which will be found preferable. Just as my first "line" forms the framework for the whole company, so the whole company, when in single rank, forms the framework for any further reinforcements. Ammunition is brought up by the rearmost "lines." By maintaining this permanent organization and depth, so strong a front is maintained that, given an equal frontage, the enemy must be forced from his position. It will be impossible for the latter, no matter in what depth his masses may be formed, to bring up sufficient rifles to gain preponderance of fire at the final stage. He may have greater numbers, but he cannot employ them; they will be merely fuel for the fire of the attack. If we recognize the immense difficulties to be overcome with only one company, what must it be for a battalion, a regiment or a brigade?

Present company training too ambitious.

Tactical schemes are studied most vigorously now by the company in all armies, but their programme is on far too large a scale. An "advance-guard" engages the enemy, a flank movement is made; one flank being threatened, a retirement is carried out, and eventually the enemy is attacked on the threatened flank. And all this on one single parade, verily a masterpiece in "tactics," of the first order! And of what use is it all? All field firing experiments are necessarily confined, and therefore we must guard against being deceived as to practical results in the field.

Fire in two directions, how obtained under proposed system.

Again in my system, if necessary, fire can be opened in two directions most easily and effectively by half lines or half companies. Fire should never be divided more than this. Officers and non-commissioned officers should of course exercise the proper amount of control, but the less the men are interfered with the better. Fire control is in itself an art, and must be exercised with the greatest care.

The double rank necessary for parade purposes.

I have urged the necessity for single rank formation, both owing to the penetration of modern rifles and the demand for the most rapid possible movements when under fire even at long ranges. All single rank formations must, however, be so organized as to admit of being massed within the shortest possible time. They must retain their "tactical" organization permanently. In short, the guiding principle must be:— Loose order in rear, and concentration to the front, both of which conditions my system complies with. Double rank formations are of course absolutely necessary for instructional and parade purposes and on my system it is exceedingly simple to form double from single rank or *vice versâ*.

The extent of future battles.

The future battle will be on an immense scale extending over several miles and lasting for several days, a frontal battle, such as the world has never yet seen, nor Military history has chronicled, a battle upon the issue of which the very existence of whole nations and countries may depend. What we require, therefore, is but few Marshalls, and a great many efficient Generals. It will no longer be a case of detached bodies engaging one another, but one big general engagement. How seldom will one corps even be able to act independently. How apparently simple its share in the battle, and yet how exceedingly difficult in reality. Woe betide the army in which leadership is deficient.

Conclusion.

I will now ask anyone who feels so disposed to work out my system. In doing so, do not be alarmed at the space required. My formations are tactically sound, and I think our imagination is apt to be cramped by seeing tactical schemes worked out on too small a scale. Since the war of 1870-71, the idea of "extended order" has gained ground, but still not to the extent demanded by modern weapons. Our ranges are far too small, our parade-grounds confined, and our manœuvres on too small a scale. Let us therefore boldly face the fact that to carry out a successful assault we *must have* a very much larger frontage. All I will ask in conclusion, is whether, in the opinion of my readers, my system can satisfactorily solve the problem of the modern Infantry attack, or at least assist in its solution in any way, and in this connection I will formulate the following questions :—

1. Does the system enable the assailants to bring their final and overwhelming fire to bear

upon the enemy at the closest and most effective range, with certainty?

2. Is the influence and supervision of commanders, so indispensable in future warfare, permanently maintained to such an extent that their plans can be carried out to the letter?

3. Does the system effectively prevent units being confused? In other words, is strict "fighting order" maintained throughout the battle?

4. Does it ensure orders being issued, and an attack being delivered simultaneously, as far at least as one brigade is concerned?

5. Does it ensure the proper supply of ammunition during the attack under all circumstances?

6. Does it place the relationship between the requirements of tactics and the occupation of cover once more on a sound footing, and does it reduce the proportion of casualties even when no cover is available?

7. Does it ensure orders being given quietly, clearly, and sensibly, and does it ensure their being carried out in satisfactory manner?

In formulating the above questions I have been actuated by a spirit of absolute impartiality. I do not claim perfection for my system in any way. If I have succeeded in merely stimulating a desire to solve a problem of such vast importance, I shall have been amply rewarded. It matters not to me personally whether the answers to my questions are "yes" or "no" but to the great matter itself it is of vital importance. I expect, therefore, a favourable criticism, as little as I fear an unfavourable one. Although personal conviction in these matters counts for a good deal, it is the established truth only to which we must give a hearing. It is surprising how eagerly we seize upon any new idea. Yet we must never be carried away by it until its efficacy has been thoroughly established. It is for critics and experts to examine and search out the truth, and to them therefore I resign my pen.

APPENDIX.

I.—GENERAL REMARKS.

In carrying out the proposed system, it is evident that it is most important that the "attack formation should be assumed at as great a distance from the enemy, or the position to be attacked as is compatible with circumstances. Otherwise modern Artillery fire is liable to very seriously affect troops when orming. Further, when once committed to a definite attack there should be little or no halting. All supports and reserves should be kept as far as possible in motion, with a view to avoiding the necessity of doubling. Thus, the first "lines," if hard pressed, will always have others arriving, fresh, and ready to resume the advance. It of course remains to be seen which system of advance most commends itself, (see page 53 of translation,) but I think most will agree that the system recommended in para. 2 (same page) will be found most advisable, that is, the "lines" passing *through* one another right up till the final or decisive zone is reached.

It is interesting to note that a system very analogous to this was proposed a short time ago by a Volunteer Officer in England, and, it is believed, was favourably criticized by the present Commander-in-Chief. As much as 26 years ago, an almost identical formation was recommended and tried, the company being formed in one rank and ordered to advance from the "right of fours," whereby four similar consecutive "lines" were formed.

The first and great objection to the proposed system will of course be its vulnerability to Artillery (Shrapnel) fire. A distinguished officer on seeing the scheme, expressed his opinion that when once Artillery got their range they would be deadly, and that such a formation as proposed, gave them the only thing they required, *viz.*, "depth."

There is of course a very great deal to be said on this point, but it may be doubtful, in the first place, whether Artillery fire would not be more or equally deadly on the *closed bodies,* which exist under the present system, than it would on *very thin dotted lines formed at such great distances* as are allowed by the proposed system. Secondly, if the moral effect, or as the author expresses it, *impetus,* of the proposed system would in any way compensate for the material drawback of giving Artillery a deeper target to aim at, it is surely worthy of consideration. Thirdly, there is the consideration, that the Artillery of the attack would presumably have something to say to that of the defence, both before the former were committed to the attack, and while the attack was being carried out.

Fourthly there is no reason why supports, or, at any rate, reserves should not be kept as long as possible under natural or extemporized cover.

Lastly, there are innumerable methods which might be suggested with a view to minimizing the effect of the enemy's artillery fire. It might even be advisable to send out yet another "line" at a great distance in advance of the firing line, say a few men, specially trained, very intelligent, and picked shots, whose duty it would be to act as "mosquitoes," to tease the enemy, draw his fire, and make him betray his dispositions, but above all to devote their attention to the *enemy's gunners.*

It is, however, scarcely necessary to discuss these and other probable suggestions. In inviting a discussion of the proposed scheme, we might add yet another rider to the author's final questions (put on page 73), somewhat after the following manner :—

"Does the system give the attack immunity from the deadly effect of Shrapnel fire, or do all its other virtues compensate for the risk incurred ?"

II.

PROPOSED ADAPTATION OF THE SCHEME.

Before proceeding to illustrate the formations for attack proposed by the author, it is as well to show the strength and composition of German units.

A German battalion has 4 companies of 200 men each, and is therefore of the same strength as a British battalion of 8 companies. As, however, the company must be preserved as an intact "fighting unit," in adapting the system to a British Battalion, it has been found necessary to increase the number of companies in the firing line, making the latter approximately as strong as in the case of a German battalion. (See Plates III and IV.)

Further, it should be noted that a German brigade has 2 regiments or 6 battalions, of 800 men each, or a total of 4,800 men, while a British brigade consists of only 3 battalions of equal strength, or a total of 2,400 only. Thus a German "regiment" (3 battalions) corresponds in strength to the British brigade.

It will be seen (Plates III and IV) that the British *battalion* has the advantage of a Reserve in hand, with almost the same fighting frontage as the German battalion, while the latter has no reserve. On the other hand, the German *brigade* has 2 battalions in reserve against only 1 battalion in the case of a british brigade. (Plates V and VI.)

In forming for attack, the author proposes that the ordinary double rank should merely "form fours," the 4 ranks thus formed opening out to the required distance as they advance. This system, it will be observed, entirely eliminates "section command," for when once the " lines " or " ranks " are set in motion, sections no longer exist intact under their original commanders, while fresh sub-units in the shape of these lines are formed under the original section commanders. I would therefore propose that each company when extending for attack, on the proposed system, should merely advance by sections from either flank as required. Each section would thus remain entirely intact until the final stage when the company is in single rank. The operation is most simple, rapid, and easy of control, either by the company commander, or section commanders individually.

It will be remembered that on page 51, it was noted that the author's meaning as regards the frontage required by a company, was somewhat obscure. With reference, therefore, to the Plates, it may be as well to explain how, it is believed, the frontages have been arrived at.

On page 69, the author states that the framework of the whole company is given from the very commencement, and that the frontage required is 120 mètres, the casualties being $\frac{1}{4}$ (see page 51). There remain, therefore, $\frac{3}{4}$ of 200 men, or 150 men to be provided for. These men are to be shoulder to shoulder when in single rank, and the company is concentrated, but are at the same time to have the fullest and freest use of their arms, etc. They would therefore occupy a full pace each, or a little more (say 33 inches). The frontage thus required is, therefore, $33'' \times 150$ men $=$ 137 yards, or roughly 120 mètres. As regards the starting point, when the company is in 4 lines, there are 50 men requiring 50 paces (intervals of 2 paces $49 \times 2 = 98$ paces) $= 148$ or, allowing full room, 150 paces, or roughly 120 mètres (130 yards). In the case of a British company we have only to halve the above measurements.

The system would be adapted to the British Infantry company in the following manner :—

"*Company Column*" on the proposed system would be adapted to an English company in double rank, thus :—

Company Commander: "Column of sections on No. 1 (or No. 4), or, "advance in column of sections from the right (or left)." "No. 1 (or No. 4) to the front, remainder form fours—left (or right)."

When completed—"by sections from the centre (or left or right) to single rank, extend."

Skirmishing Column, formed from company column.

The only order required is—"by sections from the centre (or left or right) to 3* paces extend."

"Open to—paces distancefrom No.——section."

Note.—Or this could be done from a company in ordinary double-rank formation, by merely giving the order [after No. 1 (or No. 4) to the front, remainder form fours, etc.] "By sections from the centre (or right or left) to 3 paces extend.

"*Attacking Column.*"—This can be easily formed on the above principles from either company or skirmishing column, the distances merely having to be increased between the ranks ("lines" or "sections").

---

* Or 2 paces.

"*Column of March.*"—It would be simpler to adhere to our present system of "column of route" than to adopt the author's method.

Say, the company marching in fours (left or right), is ordered to form "company column" or any of the other formations, all the orders required would be:—

"By sections—front form"—"from the centre (or left or right) to single rank (or to 3* paces) extend" (as desired), distances to be corrected on the march. The simplicity of this will at once be appreciated. A column marching along a road could at once be formed for attack without any preliminary formation, and in any direction.

A battalion would carry out the attack thus, (assuming that it is formed up in quarter-column facing the point of attack):— †

BATTALION COMMANDER'S ORDERS.

Battalion Commander: "Battalion will form for attack:

"Nos. 1, 2 and 3 companies *firing line* in 'attacking column' 2 companies to the right (or left, or one company to the right), No.——will direct. ‡

"Nos. 4, 5 and 6 companies *supports* in skirmishing column. §

"Remainder reserve."

---

* Or 2 paces.

† The same orders would apply if in column of route.

‡ Each company will then, if possible, select a point in front of their centre upon which to march.

§ These companies will of course follow exactly in rear of Nos. 1 2 and 3 respectively.

COMPANY COMMANDER'S ORDERS.

Nos. 1 *and* 4 *Company Commanders:* "Advance in column of sections from the right" (then proceed as ordered in the company drill).

Nos. 2, 3, 5 *and* 6 *Company Commanders* will then march their companies up into line (by the shortest possible way) with Nos. 1 and 4 respectively (Nos. 2 and 3 in line with No. 1, and Nos. 5 and 6 in line with No. 4) and then give the order:

"No. 4 section to the front, remainder form fours—left. (Then proceed as ordered in the company drill.) *

Intervals between companies (25 yards) can be corrected on the march, as also distances between the fighting line, supports and reserves, as decided by the battalion commander according to the nature of the ground and other circumstances. (See Plan IX.)

Of course there are innumerable details which may be worked out as regards adapting the system to ground and circumstances, but method of meeting flank, or Cavalry attacks, etc., etc. The only object in giving the above details, has been to demonstrate how very simple of management the system would be.

---

* Of course this could be varied by the order "2 companies to the left or 1 company to the right," when, in the first case, No. 1 company and No. 4 company would advance by sections left in front and Nos. 2, 3, 5 and 6 would advance in sections right in front. In the second case, Nos. 1 and 4 would advance by sections right in front, Nos. 2 and 5 will advance by sections left in front and Nos. 3 and 6 will advance by sections right in front.

Plan I.

Shewing formations proposed by Author.

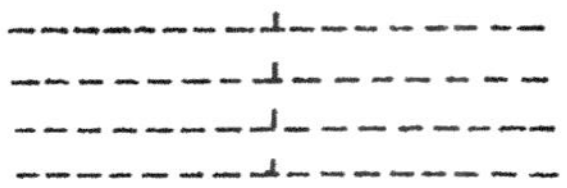

i. "*Company column.*" Company formed four-deep, all 4 ranks opened out to 25 paces distance.

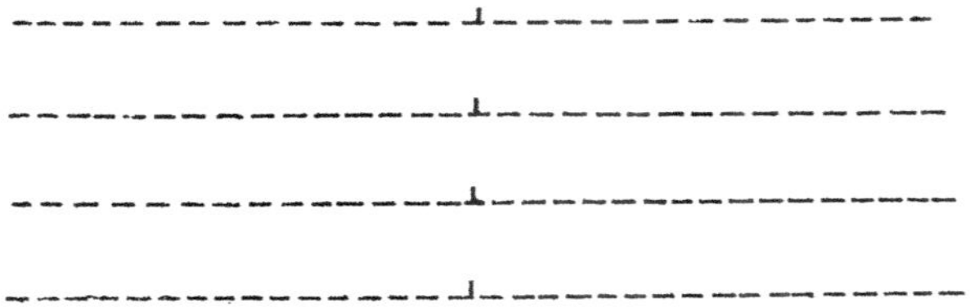

ii. "*Skirmishing column.*" Same as "company column," except that all 4 ranks are extended at 3 paces interval and distance between ranks increased to 50 paces.

iii. "*Attacking column.*" Same as "skirmishing column" with distances between ranks increased *ad lib.*

Plan II.

Shewing formations proposed by Author—(contd.)

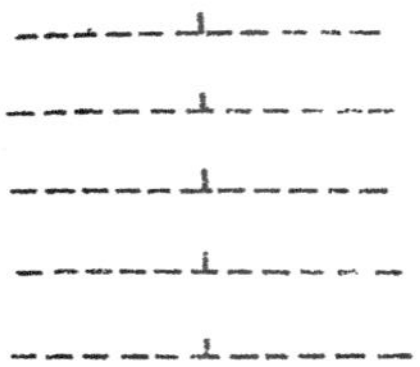

(*a*) Company column.

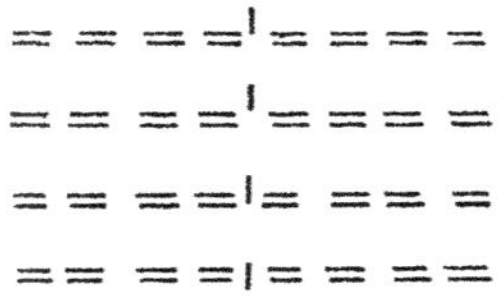

(*b*) 1st Stage.

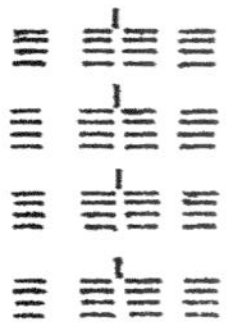

(*c*) 2nd Stage.

(*d*) 3rd Stage, "column of March."

"Column of march" formed from "company column" on the Author's system.

Plan III.

A German Battalion (4 Cos. of 200 men each) attacking.

Plan IV.

A British Battalion (8 Cos. of 100 men each) attacking.

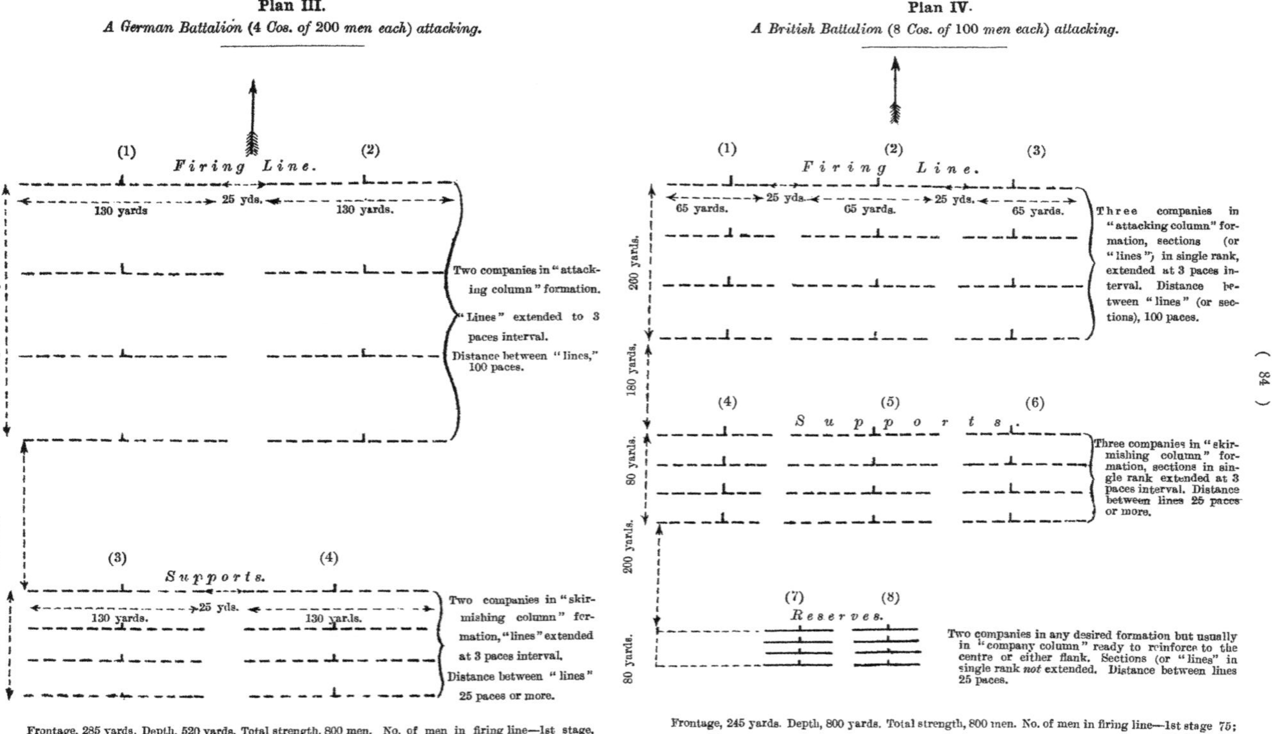

Frontage, 285 yards. Depth, 520 yards. Total strength, 800 men. No. of men in firing line—1st stage, 100; 2nd stage, 400.

Frontage, 245 yards. Depth, 800 yards. Total strength, 800 men. No. of men in firing line—1st stage 75; 2nd, stage, 300 men.

Plan V.

A German Brigade of 6 Battalions of 4 companies (of 200 men each) attacking.

Plan VI.

A British Brigade of 3 Battalions (of 8 Cos. each) attacking.

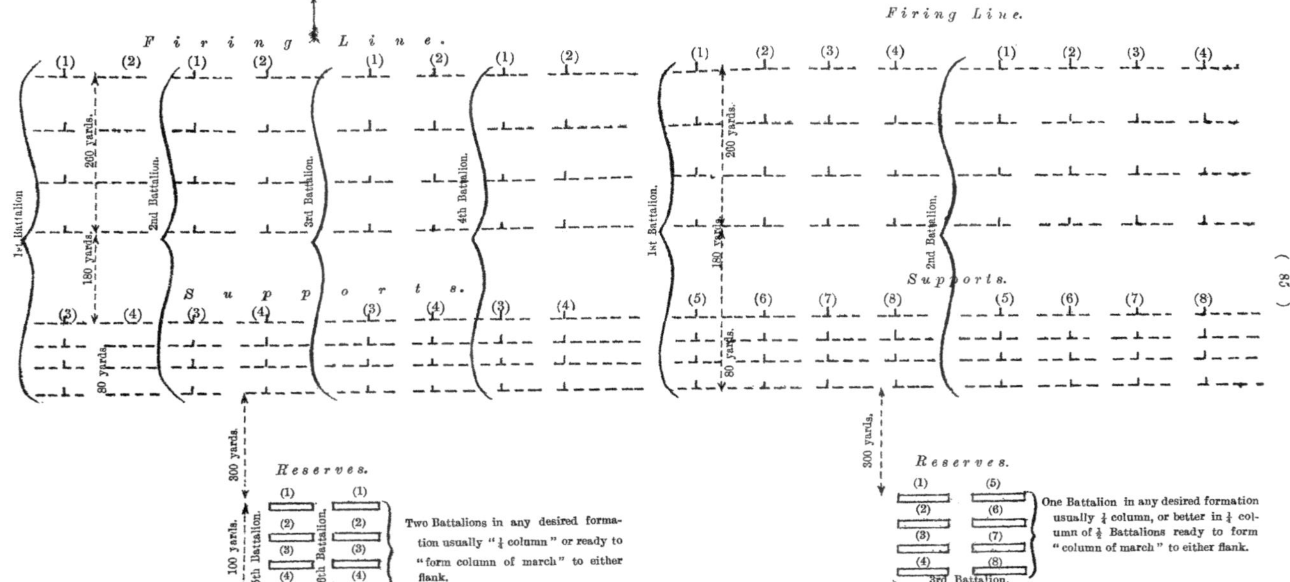

Formations of "firing line" and "supports" are the same as in the Battalion attack (each Battalion being kept intact).

Frontage about 1,200 yards. Depth about 1,000 yards. Total strength, 4,800 men. No. of men in firing line,—
... 2nd stage 1,600 men.

Formations of "firing line" and "supports" are the same as in the Battalion attack (each Battalion being kept intact).

Frontage about 700 yards. Depth about 900 yards. Total strength, 2,400 men. No. of men in firing line,—
1st stage 200 men; 2nd stage 800 men.

Plan VII.

A German Battalion (4 Companies) attacking on proposed System.

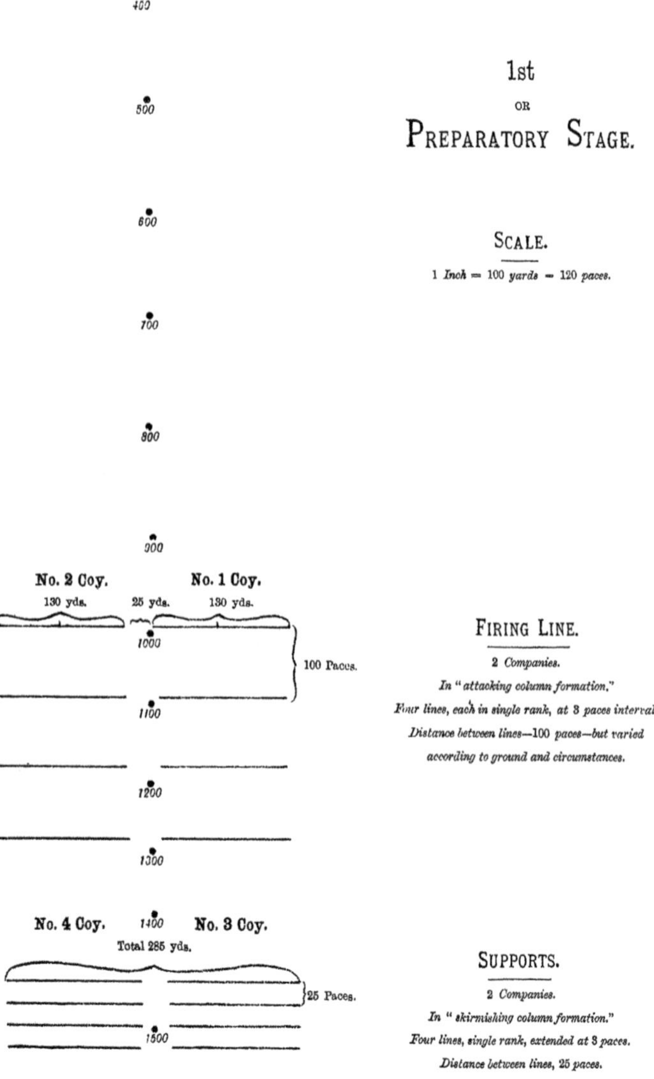

2nd or Intermediate Stage.

It will be remembered that the author recommends an advance (whenever possible) to 350 mètres (about 400 yards) without firing. If this be found impossible, then at 700 yards the 1st "rank" or "line" of the "firing line" will lie down, draw the enemy's fire, and fire themselves.

The 2nd line will meanwhile come up and pass through No. 1 and repeat this operation. Nos. 3 and 4 lines will do likewise, until the 1st line becomes the rear one, and the rear one the 1st.

If it be found necessary to increase the firing line and advance at all hazards, No. 1 lies down, waits for No. 2 to join it, when both commence firing. The two lines then advance together, seize a position, lie down and commence firing again. Meanwhile No. 3 comes up and carries Nos. 1 and and 2 with it to get another position, and in the same manner No. 4, by which time the final stage, 400 yards, should have been reached, when the decisive magazine massed fire will commence.

Plan VIII.

A German Battalion (4 Companies) attacking on proposed System.

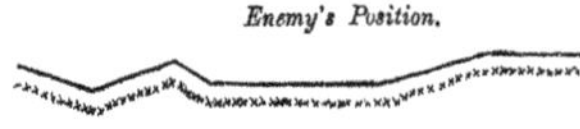

3rd
OR
FINAL STAGE.

SCALE:

1 *Inch* = 100 *yards* = 120 *paces.*

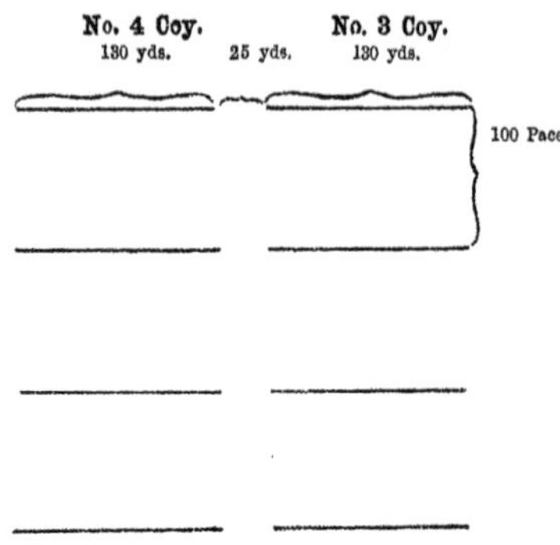

FIRING LINE.

2 *Companies.*

Single rank (shoulder-to-shoulder).

Approximate frontage, deducting ¼ *for "Casualties."*

SUPPORTS.

2 *Companies.*

In "attacking column formation."

Four lines, single rank, at 3 paces interval.

Shewing distances and changes of formation.

Plan IX.

A British Battalion forming for attack on the proposed system, shewing evolutions of each company and section.

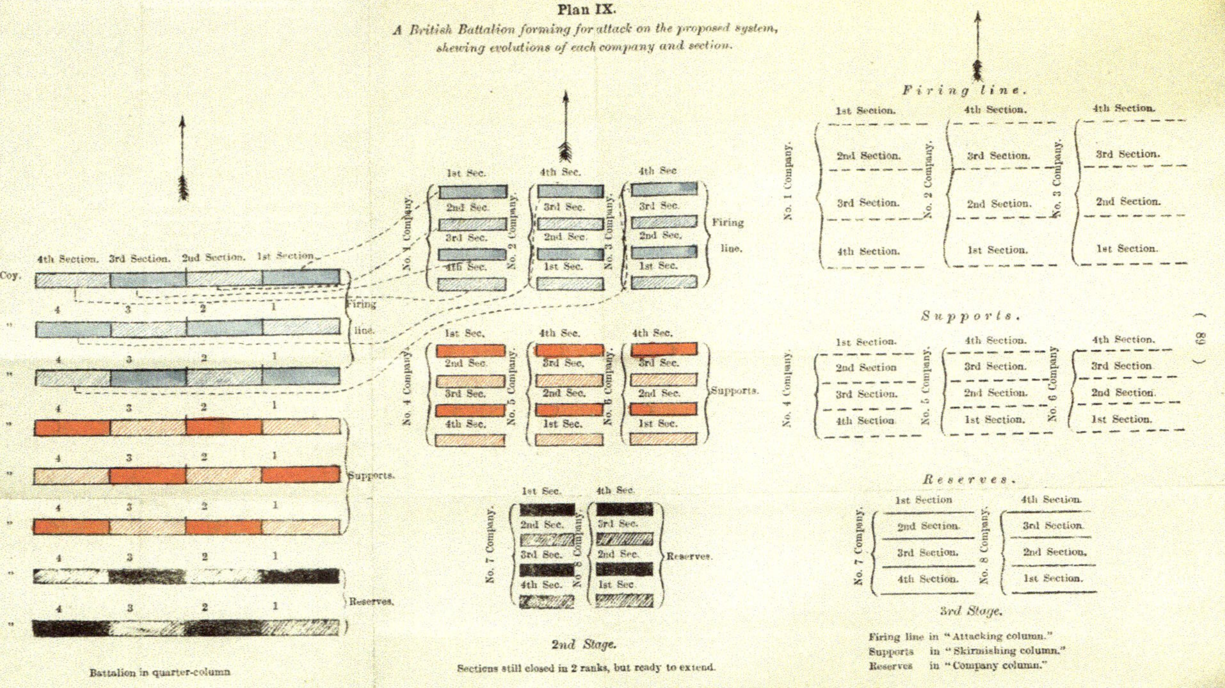

www.ingramcontent.com/pod-product-compliance
Ingram Content Group UK Ltd.
Pitfield, Milton Keynes, MK11 3LW, UK
UKHW021835270726
14058UKWH00002B/166

9 781847 348579